Gardening to Attract Birds & Butterflies

WRITER
PEGGY HENRY

PHOTOGRAPHER
SAXON HOLT

ILLUSTRATOR
JAMES BALKOVEK

LAWN & GARDEN

Product Manager: CYNTHIA FOLLAND, NK LAWN & GARDEN CO.

Acquisition, Development and Production Services: JENNINGS & KEEFE: Media Development, Corte Madera, CA

Acquisition: JACK JENNINGS, BOB DOLEZAL

Series Concept: BOB DOLEZAL

Project Director: JILL FOX

Developmental Editor: CYNTHIA PUTNAM

Horticultural Consultant: RG TURNER JR

Ornithology Consultant: STEVE HOWELL

Photographic Director: SAXON HOLT

Art Director (interior): BRAD GREENE

Cover Designer: KAREN EMERSON

Page Make-up: BRAD GREENE

Copy Editor: VIRGINIA RICH

Proofreader: LYNN FERAR

Indexer: SYLVIA COATES

Photo Assistant: PEGGY HENRY

Additional Photographers: Pages 42-43 (Starting Seed Indoors) Alan Copeland and Barry Shapiro; Pages 46-47 and 62-63 Maslowski Wildlife Productions

Color Separations: PREPRESS ASSEMBLY INCORPORATED

Printing and Binding: WOLFER PRINTING COMPANY

PRINTED IN THE USA

Cover: Striking orange and black monarch butterflies are a common sight on purple coneflowers, *Echinacea purpurea,* in late summer.

This page: Monarchs overwinter by massing on the branches of trees.

First Edition

Library of Congress Cataloging-in-Publication Data:
Henry, Peggy
    Gardening to attract birds & butterflies / writer,
  Peggy Henry ; photographer, Saxon Holt ; illustrator,
James Balkovek.
        p. cm.
    Includes index.
    ISBN 1-880281-17-1 (pbk.)
    1. Gardening to attract birds. 2. Butterfly gardening.
  I. Henry, Peggy, 1956- . II. Holt, Saxon.
  QL676.5.G36 1994
  635.9' 6 -- dc20   94-34534
                                                            CIP

Special thanks to: Valerie Brown; Theo Crawford; Coyote Point Museum, San Mateo, CA; Annie Fisher; Louise Hallberg; Polly Holt; Sandy Maillard; Dorothy Orr; John Rumph; Janet Sanchez; Sonoma Mission Gardens, Sonoma, CA; Katie Trefethen

95   96   97   10   9   8   7   6   5   4   3   2   1

TABLE OF CONTENTS

Welcoming Birds & Butterflies 4–5
Advantages of Colorful Visitors 6–7
Creating a Bird & Butterfly Garden 8–9
Attracting Birds 10–11
Trees for Birds 12–13
Shrubs for Birds 14–15
Vines & Ground Covers for Birds 16–17
Flowers for Birds 18–19
Berries for Birds 20–21
Encouraging Nesting 22–23
Attracting Butterflies 24–25
Life Cycle of the Butterfly 26–27
Nectar-Rich Flowers 28–29
Shrubs for Butterflies 30–31
Trees & Grasses for Butterflies 32–33
Feeding Caterpillars 34–35
Garden Design 36–37
A Sample Garden 38–39
Improving the Soil 40–41
Installing Plants 42–43
Maintaining the Garden 44–45
Seasonal Care 46–47
Solving Problems 48–49
Water in the Garden 50–51
Creating a Backyard Pond 52–53
Building a Birdhouse 54–55
Growing a Birdhouse 56–57
Feeding Birds 58–59
Observing Birds 60–61
Common Birds 62–63
Attracting Hummingbirds 64–65
Identifying Butterflies 66–67
Common Butterflies 68–69
Raising Butterflies 70–71
Going Beyond the Garden 72–73
Plant Reference Chart 74–77
Index 78–79
A Note from NK Lawn & Garden 80

WELCOMING BIRDS & BUTTERFLIES

A GARDEN TO SHARE

A beautiful, blooming garden is a celebration of life. Birds and butterflies contribute to its charm and vitality by adding color, movement and in some cases song.

For a garden to attract birds or butterflies, it must have adequate sources of food, shelter and water. At first glance, such a landscape may not seem different from any other. On closer inspection, you'll find that the plants and other elements have been carefully chosen to meet a variety of needs. Flowers provide nectar and seeds. Shrubs and trees make berries or fruit. And other plantings serve as greenery for caterpillars. These and other plants also offer shelter, breeding places and nesting sites. Ponds, fountains or other water elements accent the garden and provide necessary moisture.

A garden that attracts wildlife often has a looser, more natural appearance than a formally landscaped garden, which requires careful manicuring. Dried flowers, spilled seeds and fallen leaves are all part of this natural look and help support the feeding and nesting activities of your visitors. And by avoiding pesticides or herbicides, which can harm birds and butterflies, you'll attract other animals and beneficial insects that may have been missing from your yard for some time.

Remember that birds and butterflies will come to depend on the food and shelter in your garden, especially during the winter. Your reward for providing a backyard haven will be an up close view of these fascinating creatures all year long.

Shrubs add interest and provide food and shelter throughout the year.

Water elements are a vital resource to visitors. They also serve as focal points within the garden.

Trees lend structure to the garden and provide nesting sites for birds and butterflies.

USING THIS BOOK

With the help of this book, you will be able to plan and create a backyard garden where colorful birds and butterflies bring their delights into close range. Discover which garden elements attract birds and butterflies and find out how to incorporate them—whether you want to create a new garden or simply add to an existing landscape.

In step-by-step fashion, see how to prepare a garden plan, improve soil, install and maintain plants and solve pest and disease problems using natural methods. Descriptions and photographs of many kinds of plants—from trees and shrubs to flowers, ground covers, vines and grasses—help you choose outstanding varieties that are easy to grow and attract birds and butterflies. The handy Plant Reference Chart on pages 74–77 shows you information at a glance on the trees, shrubs, flowers, vines and ground covers that are described in the book.

Learn how to create a small backyard pond, build a wooden birdhouse and raise butterflies in a simple homemade cage. Other sections cover using water elements in the garden, feeding birds, attracting hummingbirds and visiting public gardens and information centers.

Photographs and text highlight birds and butterflies common throughout North America and describe which plantings will attract them. Tips on observation techniques and on using field guides and equipment help you identify the species that do visit the garden.

With a basic understanding of what kind of garden attracts birds and butterflies, and by using the specific, step-by-step methods in this book, you'll be able to create a garden of any size for all of your guests to enjoy.

Colorful annual and perennial flowers provide seeds and nectar.

ADVANTAGES OF COLORFUL VISITORS

BENEFITS OF BUTTERFLIES

If you've ever watched a boldly patterned red admiral butterfly as it lights and dances among bright, fragrant flowers, you know how captivating these creatures can be. For their entertainment value alone, butterflies are well worth attracting to the garden.

Besides their delicate beauty, butterflies have much to offer. Butterflies provide a valuable service by pollinating flowers. Pollen from the flower sticks to the butterfly's legs and is transferred onto different flowers as the butterfly moves around and feeds. This spreading of pollen starts seed production in the flower and keeps the plant's life cycle going.

Visiting butterflies offer excellent opportunities for nature study. You can get very close to butterflies to watch as they drink nectar, warm their wings in the sun or even lay eggs on leaves. Witnessing the emergence of a brilliant butterfly from its chrysalis is simply unforgettable. And, children find them fascinating.

From a conservation standpoint, a butterfly garden promotes the survival of local butterfly populations, which benefits the overall environment. In an age when open land is being lost to development or damaged by herbicides and pesticides, a backyard preserve is an important sanctuary. In return for sharing your garden with these beautiful creatures and their hungry offspring, you'll receive a front row seat for one of nature's best shows.

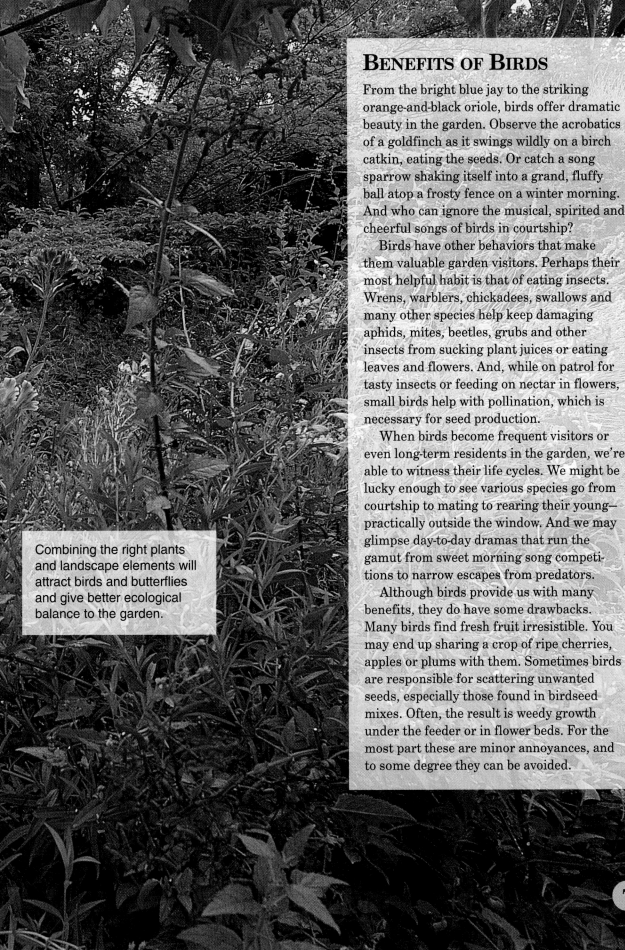

Combining the right plants and landscape elements will attract birds and butterflies and give better ecological balance to the garden.

BENEFITS OF BIRDS

From the bright blue jay to the striking orange-and-black oriole, birds offer dramatic beauty in the garden. Observe the acrobatics of a goldfinch as it swings wildly on a birch catkin, eating the seeds. Or catch a song sparrow shaking itself into a grand, fluffy ball atop a frosty fence on a winter morning. And who can ignore the musical, spirited and cheerful songs of birds in courtship?

Birds have other behaviors that make them valuable garden visitors. Perhaps their most helpful habit is that of eating insects. Wrens, warblers, chickadees, swallows and many other species help keep damaging aphids, mites, beetles, grubs and other insects from sucking plant juices or eating leaves and flowers. And, while on patrol for tasty insects or feeding on nectar in flowers, small birds help with pollination, which is necessary for seed production.

When birds become frequent visitors or even long-term residents in the garden, we're able to witness their life cycles. We might be lucky enough to see various species go from courtship to mating to rearing their young—practically outside the window. And we may glimpse day-to-day dramas that run the gamut from sweet morning song competitions to narrow escapes from predators.

Although birds provide us with many benefits, they do have some drawbacks. Many birds find fresh fruit irresistible. You may end up sharing a crop of ripe cherries, apples or plums with them. Sometimes birds are responsible for scattering unwanted seeds, especially those found in birdseed mixes. Often, the result is weedy growth under the feeder or in flower beds. For the most part these are minor annoyances, and to some degree they can be avoided.

CREATING A BIRD & BUTTERFLY GARDEN

ATTRACTING VISITORS

A bird and butterfly garden is always evolving. This overview outlines some of the phases in the process; detailed information follows later in the book.

Begin by determining which species live in your area. Observe the wildlife already in the yard and visit neighboring gardens, parks and open fields. Consult field guides to identify individual species and the food and shelter plants they prefer.

Next set personal goals. Consider what elements make the landscape most pleasing to you. Perhaps you want trees for fall color or plants that bloom over many seasons.

Decide on a site. Sunny areas will attract many birds and butterflies, but shady areas are better for birds that prefer woodland settings. The site should be accessible and allow easy viewing. It should be big enough to meet your goals and accommodate the plants on your list.

Measure the area and draw up a simple base plan. Experiment with different combinations of plants and other elements such as pathways, seating areas or water accents. Once you've decided on the right arrangement, sketch a more detailed plan. Install elements such as ponds, pathways or seating areas first.

Before you plant, prepare the soil to get the plants off to a good start. Have a soil sample tested to determine which amendments will boost soil fertility. Sow seeds or install plants, and perform routine maintenance as the garden grows and matures. After a year, the garden should begin to fill in, although plants will not yet be mature enough to completely fill spaces. Plant annuals to fill in the gaps and add color.

Installation & Care

Site Selection Choosing the right site is the first step to a successful garden. It need not be a large space, since a few plants in a sunny section of the yard may attract many species. Consider exposure to sun or wind, soil type and maintenance.

Design In the design process let your creative side take over. Experimenting with the plan helps you to place plants where they will flourish and complement other elements. You may find the plan changes several times before you're satisfied with the design.

Soil Preparation Preparing the soil before you plant helps plants grow vigorously. Adding amendments such as compost, garden waste or well-rotted manure enriches poor soils and improves drainage in heavy soils. Dig materials deeply to reach root zones.

Adding Special Features Consider adding a birdhouse, a bird feeder or a special basin to collect water. These and other extras such as ponds and cages to raise butterflies help meet food, water and shelter needs and aid conservation efforts.

Maintenance Routine maintenance such as watering, fertilizing and pruning will help the garden thrive. Letting some flowers go to seed and leaving debris for nesting material benefits many birds. Butterflies will drink from puddles left by watering or rain.

Letting the Garden Evolve Even before your garden completely grows in, you will be rewarded by visits from many species of birds and butterflies. You can fill in gaps with annuals, but allow the garden to mature before adding more shrubs or larger plants.

Attracting Birds

Food & Water

Attract birds to the garden with an assortment of plants and other elements that provide food and water.

Birds live on seeds, insects, fruits (including berries), nuts and nectar. When planning, consider plants that produce food in all seasons, especially winter and early spring when natural food sources are scarce.

Seeds provide a primary diet for many birds, including sparrows, finches, doves, grosbeaks and cardinals. The graceful birch you choose for fall color and summer shade becomes a wonderful food source when dangling catkins spill tiny seeds. A flower border of aster, columbine, coreopsis, cosmos, zinnias and sunflowers will add dazzling color to your garden and draw many songbirds when it goes to seed.

You and the birds will enjoy spring blooms from fruit trees and winter berries from many shrubs, including cotoneaster, viburnum and holly. Dogwood, crabapple and hawthorn trees offer form, spring color and bountiful fruit.

Insects on elm, sycamore, willow and maple trees will attract chickadees, wrens, warblers and many other birds. Sweet nectar, often found in popular garden flowers such as fuchsia, salvia, lantana, bee balm and phlox, will attract hummingbirds.

Small ponds, decorative fountains or birdbaths provide water and double as focal points in the garden. Birds also bathe and drink in sprinklers, saucers, pots and even mud puddles.

When planning for food and water elements, locate birdbaths and feeders in open areas away from fences, rooftops and shrubs that hide predators, especially cats.

Viburnum, which offers colorful berries and shelter for birds, works well in hedge, screen and foundation plantings.

SHELTER REQUIREMENTS

Refuge from the elements or from prowling predators is as important as adequate food and water. Providing shelter with a variety of trees, shrubs, vines and hedges will enhance the landscape and offer the diversity necessary for protection in all seasons.

Groupings of pine, fir or other evergreen trees are excellent sanctuaries in harsh weather. Trees add stately elegance to the landscape and can be planted for privacy or as screens, although some may grow slowly. In mild regions, broadleaf evergreens such as the flowering tea tree, *Leptospermum* species, or evergreen pear, *Pyrus kawakamii*, are effective.

Shrubs provide hiding places, shady resting spots and quick cover from predators. For the best protection, let shrubs and undergrowth grow into a tangle or thicket in an out-of-the-way area of the yard. Attractive mixed shrub plantings, especially thorny varieties, offer great cover and make an effective background for flower beds or lawns.

Some excellent shrubs can be found in the barberry family, which includes deciduous and evergreen plants of many sizes. Tough and drought-tolerant, plants from this group display excellent foliage color and berries. The Japanese barberry variety *Berberis vulgaris* 'Atropurpurea' has bronzy red to purple foliage in the spring and summer and bright red berries in the winter.

Vines on fences or trellises offer quick cover for birds. Honeysuckle vines are an exceptional choice because of their fast growth, masses of twiggy stems and sheltering foliage. Boston ivy works well too.

Another option for shelter in the garden is a hedge. Hedges preserve privacy, reduce noise, block unwanted views and frame certain areas or features of the yard. Small boxwood hedges provide birds with protection practically at ground level, while large privet or holly hedges can reach 20 feet.

TREES FOR BIRDS

A PLACE TO PERCH

Trees are dominant elements in the landscape and the foundation of a garden that attracts birds. For people they offer shade and beauty; for birds they supply fruit, seeds, sap, insects, shelter and nesting sites.

A stately Colorado spruce, for example, lends form and texture to the garden while providing shelter and nesting places for visitors. On a smaller scale, the dwarf Alberta spruce and other varieties of dwarf spruce trees offer the same features but grow more slowly—to a maximum of about ten feet. These and other evergreen trees are important choices for winter color and protection.

If it's brilliant fall foliage you want, try deciduous trees, which double as seed and insect sources. Maples are graceful deciduous trees ranging from small Japanese maples suitable for containers to the red maple of 60 feet or more. Maples also provide good shelter and nesting sites.

For color in the landscape, consider the many fruit trees that are among the first plants to bloom each spring. Look for disease-resistant varieties and don't be put off by a lack of space. Many excellent dwarf or semi-dwarf selections are available. Birds will be attracted to most fruit crops, in some cases taking more than their share. To save some of the crop for yourself, cover part of the tree with netting or hang shiny metal lids or foil strips from the branches.

When you choose a tree, make sure that you have the space, soil and exposure to meet its needs. Consider spread, height and growth habits—a deciduous tree that shades the house in summer may become a nuisance in fall if its dropping leaves clog drains or gutters.

For planting instructions, see pages 42-43.

Fruit trees, like this Gravenstein apple, mark the seasons beautifully with spring blossoms, summer shade and autumn color. Fruit draws many birds, including orioles and cardinals. Pears, peaches, plums, cherries and figs are also excellent choices.

Nut trees, like this black walnut, *Juglans nigra,* are large landscape trees that can be used for shade and screening. Their nuts are eaten by woodpeckers, jays, nuthatches and others. Many of these trees, including oak, hickory, pecan and beech, attract insects and provide birds with shelter.

Broadleaf evergreen trees, like this southern magnolia, *Magnolia grandiflora,* are prized for their year-round greenery and pleasing form. They provide flowers, berries, winter shelter and nesting sites and attract robins, mockingbirds and catbirds.

Deciduous trees, like this European white birch, *Betula pendula,* make graceful showpieces, groupings or screen plantings. Many attract juncos, jays, finches, orioles, warblers and others. Sycamore, liquidambar and willow are other good choices.

Conifers or needled evergreen trees, including this Colorado blue spruce, *Picea pungens* 'Glauca', will keep the landscape from looking barren in winter and serve as beautiful backdrops to other plantings. They draw chickadees, goldfinches, grosbeaks and woodpeckers.

Flowering trees, like evergreen pear, tulip tree and this crape myrtle, *Lagerstroemia indica,* add outstanding garden color and make dramatic specimens. Many produce seeds and nectar and also attract insects. They draw hummingbirds, cardinals, finches, grosbeaks and others.

SHRUBS FOR BIRDS

TWO IN THE BUSH

Shrubs provide seeds, nectar, berries and insects for birds as well as shelter and nesting sites and materials. As individuals or in groups, shrubs offer a variety of sizes, shapes and textures. They're useful for creating privacy, as backdrops for other plantings, or as accents. Shrubs help create a unified look in the garden by establishing themes and leading the eye to various garden elements.

Shrubs offer colorful flowers and fruit that help feed birds over many seasons. Bush honeysuckle shrubs are very attractive to birds. Hardy Tatarian honeysuckle, with fragrant flowers in late spring and red berries in summer, is a fine selection.

Shrubs are often used as foundation plantings to set off the beauty of a home. Evergreen choices such as mahonia, bayberry or heavenly bamboo look good all year and offer berries, insects and nesting material.

Use smaller shrubs to complement flower borders or to lead the eye gradually from the lawn to larger background plantings. Winter creeper (*Euonymus fortunei*) varieties such as 'Greenlane' with orange berry-like fruit and 'Emerald Gaiety' with green fruit are good examples of attractive, versatile small shrubs.

Be sure to consider height and spread when selecting shrubs, and allow enough growing space. Resist the temptation to fill in an area by putting shrubs closer together than recommended. You may be disappointed as the plants grow and begin looking crowded. When planting groupings, be aware of foliage color and texture. In general, plant finely textured shrubs in front of more coarsely textured ones to maintain a unified look. For more planting information, see pages 42–43.

Lilacs provide birds with early spring buds, nectar-rich flowers, insects and excellent nesting sites.

Flowering shrubs, like the edible early spring buds of golden bells, *Forsythia* x *intermedia,* make excellent accent plants while providing exceptional nesting sites. Many offer flowers with nectar for hummingbirds (fuchsia), late spring blooms (mock orange) and late season berries (viburnum). Flowering shrubs are also useful as hedges, as background and foundation plantings and along borders. Expect sparrows, finches, towhees, cedar waxwings, mockingbirds and robins to visit.

Deciduous shrubs make up a large group and include this Japanese or shrub rose, with fragrant, long-blooming flowers that develop into edible rose hips enjoyed by cardinals, robins, chickadees and others. Many birds find shelter and nesting sites within the rose bush, which turns a bright red in the   fall. Choose deciduous shrubs for accents, borders, containers, hedges or screens. Forsythia, rugosa rose, azalea and spiraea are excellent choices.

Fruiting shrubs, such as this pyracantha, *Pyracantha angustifolia,* provide color and food throughout the year. Fruiting shrubs range from ground covers to large plants and are used as barriers, screens, hedges and foundation plantings and accents. Some berries may be intoxicating to birds, others are poisonous to humans; if this is a concern ask a knowledgeable person about the specific plant you intend to purchase.

Evergreen shrubs, such as this Pfitzer juniper, *Juniperus chinensis* 'Pfitzerana,' are neat, often symmetrical plants that hold foliage and form throughout the year, making them ideal for cover and nesting. Evergreen shrubs are useful as screens, barriers, foundation plantings, hedges and backgrounds. Some, including holly, privet, mahonia and juniper, provide fruit enjoyed by bluebirds, mockingbirds, warblers, waxwings, robins and flickers.

VINES & GROUND COVERS FOR BIRDS

ADDING NEW DIMENSIONS

Climbing vines and low ground covers add dimension to a landscape, help unify elements of varying heights and soften the hard lines of houses and other structures. They also entice birds with flowers, berries, insects, shelter and nesting sites.

Honeysuckle is one of the best all-around vines, valued for its fragrant late spring flowers, black autumn berries and vigorous stems. These easy-to-grow plants tolerate many soils and reliably cover fences, trellises, banks and walls.

Grape is another very satisfactory vine for summer shade, fall fruit and foliage color and interesting branch patterns. Blackbirds, jays, cardinals, waxwings, orioles and many other birds will help with the harvest.

Use vines to cover unsightly fences, walls and rocks. For vines growing along the house, install trellises a few inches away from the walls to protect them from dampness.

Ground covers are key features in any landscape because they make the transition from lawns to shrubs or trees seem natural. Many are good for shady areas where nothing else thrives. They are excellent choices for erosion control, for filling in areas where lawns would be difficult to mow and for concealing leaf litter below trees.

Low-growing junipers and ivy are good evergreen ground covers, providing excellent cover and nesting sites for birds. Coralberry, *Symphoricarpos orbiculatus,* with purple-red berries, grows well on slopes and can be used for erosion control, as can prostrate rosemary and chokeberry.

Honesuckle vines, *Lonicera* species, offer a bounty of nectar, fruit, insects and nesting sites and attract many species.

Annual vines, like this cardinal climber, *Ipomoea quamoclit,* provide quick, short-term color and temporary cover for trellises, fences or arbors. These vines, including morning glory, scarlet runner bean and sweet pea, offer nectar for hummingbirds and shelter for many small birds. Plant seeds after danger of frost has passed or start them indoors several weeks earlier.

Evergreen ground covers are perfect choices for erosion control on hillsides or for areas where you need neat, green carpets of foliage, as this mock strawberry, *Duchesnea indica,* demonstrates. The thick tangle of leafy branches provides cover and nesting for many small birds, including towhees, house finches and sparrows. This strawberry provides fruit, flowers and insects.

Perennial vines, such as this colorful summer trumpet vine, *Campsis radicans,* are useful for long-term screens over upright supports where they provide good cover for birds. Hummingbirds and orioles are attracted to the trumpet vine flowers, and chickadees and goldfinches take seeds from the pods in winter. Fragrant wisteria flowers in spring attract hummingbirds, as do the bright but tender flower bracts of the bougainvillea.

Ornamental grasses, such as this sheep's fescue, *Festuca amethystina,* are perfect choices for low maintenance areas and make striking accents in the garden. The wide selection of available varieties offer a range of leaf colors and textures, flowers and growth habits from loose to manicured. Dense clumps of grasses provide seed for eating as well as cover and resting zones for many small birds including sparrows and towhees.

FLOWERS FOR BIRDS

ANNUALS & PERENNIALS

Flowers are usually the brightest stars of the garden, delighting the senses with fragrance and color. Annuals and perennials also play critical roles in supplying birds with seeds and nectar.

Annuals are plants that live, flower and die in one year. They're perfect for color among perennials or shrubs. Many annuals are easy to grow. Sow seeds outdoors in prepared soil after the danger of frost has passed. Or start them indoors several weeks earlier. For quick garden color, set out the young transplants that are available at nurseries or garden centers during each growing season.

Carnations, four o'clocks and lobelia attract hummingbirds. If left to go to seed, many annuals, including ageratum, aster, coreopsis, scabiosa, cleome and California poppy, provide food for small birds such as goldfinches, sparrows and towhees.

Perennials are nonwoody plants that live at least three years. With some perennials, the foliage dies back in winter but the roots stay alive and send up new growth the following spring. These plants form clumps of foliage and most provide wonderful floral displays. Perennials can be started from seed or transplants. Hummingbirds feed on the nectar of penstemon, phlox, bee balm, columbine, coral bells and salvia. Seed-producing perennials include goldenrod, coreopsis and globe thistle.

Plant annuals and perennials in beds and borders or in small groupings to punctuate an area of the garden. Position low flowers in front of taller ones. Follow traditional color schemes or simply mix colors that appeal to you.

Annuals

Bachelor's button, *Centaurea cyanus,* is a hardy 1–3 ft. tall plant with bright blue, pink or white flowers. The seeds attract many birds, especially finches.

Cosmos, *Cosmos bipinnatus and C. sulphureus,* are excellent garden flowers with a long bloom time and a variety of colors. The seeds attract goldfinches.

Marigolds, *Tagetes erecta,* are reliable plants with bright flowers in warm colors— yellow, orange, maroon or bicolors. Plants range from 6 in. to 3 ft. and are easy to start from seed.

18

Nasturtiums, *Tropaeolum majus,* are climbers or low, mounding plants, with brilliant red, pink, yellow, orange or coral flowers that attract hummingbirds.

Sunflowers, *Helianthus annuus,* provide a feast of seeds on tall background plants that reach 6–12 ft. Seeds attract finches, sparrows, jays and others.

Zinnias, *Zinnia elegans,* have it all—incredible color (every shade except blue), a size range from 6 in. to 3 ft., ease of cultivation, flowers over a long season and seeds that attract birds.

Perennials

Coral bells, *Heuchera sanguinea,* offer drifts of dainty coral, pink, white or red nodding, bell-shaped flowers that attract hummingbirds and small insects.

Coreopsis, *Coreopsis verticillata,* is a drought-tolerant perennial and adds spark to summer gardens. Finches, sparrows and others eat the seeds.

Delphiniums, *Delphinium* hybrids, offer striking blue, red, pink, lavender or purple flowers on tall spikes. Easily grown from seed, these perennials attract hummingbirds.

Goldenrod, *Solidago* species, sends up soft yellow plumes from mounded plants. Insects are attracted to the flowers, which feed many birds if left to go to seed.

Bee balm, *Monarda didyma,* has mint-scented foliage and large clusters of tubular flowers. The red, pink or lavender flowers attract hummingbirds.

Columbine, *Aquilegia* species, is prized for its graceful spring flowers in blue-and-white, red-and-yellow and pink, purple, cream and lilac. Hummingbirds like the flowers; small birds eat the seeds.

BERRIES FOR BIRDS

Berries are an essential food source for many birds and can be found on trees, shrubs, vines and ground covers. As the attractive berries and foliage on this cotoneaster, *Cotoneaster* species, illustrate, many berry plants make outstanding garden specimens.

Shrubs, such as this handsome autumn-fruiting viburnum, *Viburnum plicatum tomentosum*, make up the largest category of berry-producing plants. Viburnums are noteworthy for their attractive foliage and sometimes fragrant flowers in addition to the long-lasting bright red to black berries preferred by bluebirds, waxwings, cardinals, sparrows and robins. Viburnum shrubs are perfect as accent, foundation and mixed border plants. Several are shade tolerant.

Versatile cotoneaster shrubs and ground covers attract both hummingbirds, which visit the spring flowers, and birds that eat berries. Rock cotoneaster, shown here, is a ground cover.

Cane berries like this loganberry, *Rubus ursinus*, are the favorite food in summer of over 100 birds, including jays, mockingbirds, cardinals and orioles. Vigorous spreaders, cane berries need containment in many garden settings, although if left to grow into a thicket, they provide top-notch nesting sites. Cane berries, which include blackberries, raspberries and loganberries, are best grown on large lots where they can go "wild." The roots are invasive.

Trees that produce berries, such as this Washington thorn, *Crataegus phaenopyrum,* shown in winter, often offer late-season fruit that follows spring flowers. While its berries are an important food source to waxwings, grosbeaks, jays, robins and scores of other birds, the Washington thorn also attracts insects for chickadees, warblers and others. Its thorny branches offer good cover.

Ground covers that produce berries, like this manzanita, *Arctostaphylos* species, are perfect complements to lawns, shrubs and flowers. These neat, easy, slightly mounding plants trail beautifully over hillsides and fall over walls. Pretty white flowers in late winter or early spring are followed by bright red berries that attract towhees, sparrows, jays, grosbeaks and mockingbirds. Other ground covers include varieties of natal plum, juniper and barberry.

FOOD FOR ALL SEASONS

As autumn turns to winter and the supply of seeds and insects dwindles, berries become a primary food source for many backyard birds, including robins, chickadees, nuthatches, sparrows, warblers and waxwings. They are an important part of the spring and summer diet as well. Planting trees, shrubs and ground covers so that there are berries in every season will attract birds and provide color year-round.

Many plants that produce berries have wonderful flowers or autumn foliage. Various species make excellent specimen trees, accent shrubs, massed ground covers or vines.

Winter berries that hold well into the season are critical. Firethorn, or, pyracantha is a classic example, bearing brilliant orange or red berries over many months. These thorny shrubs work well as barriers, background plants and fall accents. Other fine plants for winter berries include nandina, photinia, holly, barberry and viburnum. For trees consider red cedar, crabapple and hawthorn.

With the arrival of spring, many migrating birds and resident species will enjoy February daphne, with bright red berries in May, or the white mulberry, a fast-growing tree with white flowers and pale pink berries.

Summer berries are abundant on native serviceberries, which grow as shrubs or small trees with showy white flowers, beautiful autumn foliage and interesting branch patterns. Alder buckthorn, elderberry and coffeeberry plants are other good choices.

Flowering dogwood, a beautiful, graceful spring-blooming tree, heads the list for fall berry producers, followed by the Japanese dogwood, *Cornus kousa,* and the alternate-leaved dogwood, with its bright blue berries. Mountain ash, crabapple and autumn olive are other excellent species for fall berries.

Be aware that some berries can be poisonous to humans. Choose nonpoisonous varieties if this is a concern.

ENCOURAGING NESTING

Offering safe areas for breeding and nesting helps sustain and even increase bird populations. A number of trees, shrubs and ground covers make good nesting sites and provide materials for nest building.

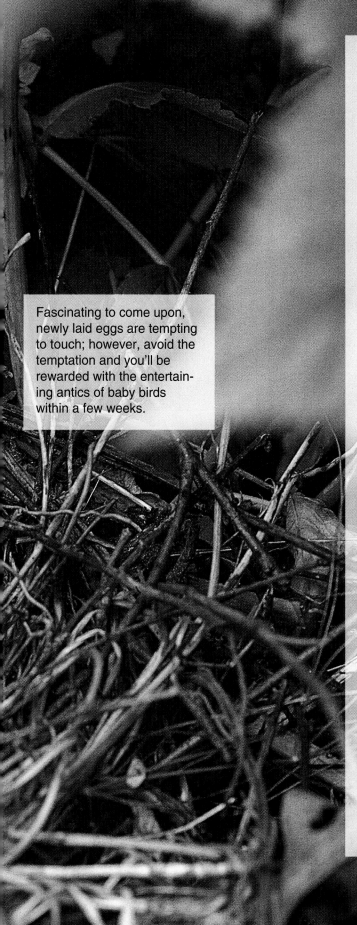

Fascinating to come upon, newly laid eggs are tempting to touch; however, avoid the temptation and you'll be rewarded with the entertaining antics of baby birds within a few weeks.

NEW RESIDENTS

Birds nest in many places—inside cavities, on ledges, on the ground and in the foliage of plants. The key to meeting nesting needs is to offer a landscape with many choices.

To lure cavity and ledge nesting birds such as swallows, wrens and woodpeckers, birdhouses and trees with natural hollows work well. Birds that nest on the ground will look for areas away from noise and foot traffic.

Birds that nest in trees, shrubs, woody vines and ground covers will be the most likely to build backyard homes. The nests will be as varied as the species who build them. The cardinal chooses deep, dense shrubbery, the oriole suspends a nest from branch tips and many birds select inner branches and V-shaped limb junctions for nesting.

Trees that have been known to host many species include apple, elm, hawthorn, maple, oak, pine, red cedar and willow. These trees attract robins, finches, sparrows, jays, cardinals, towhees, catbirds and many others. Include trees of different ages. Some birds, such as the goldfinch, prefer young trees for nesting, while orioles and robins are more likely to nest in mature trees.

Shrubs and vines that offer good nesting sites are juniper, rose, lilac, dogwood, privet, barberry, honeysuckle, forsythia, grape, pyracantha, mock orange, climbing rose and wisteria. Prune shrubs moderately. Vines provide homes for mockingbirds, hummingbirds and cardinals.

Nesting materials include items that camouflage—moss, lichen and plant debris—and household items, such as string and bits of paper. Allowing some twigs, grass and other debris to collect in the garden will give birds a good selection of materials to use for nest building. Some birds, such as barn and cliff swallows, use wet mud to build their nests. Encourage them to nest by setting a shallow pan of mud in a corner of the yard. Keep the mud moist.

ATTRACTING BUTTERFLIES

Butterflies, with their delightful grace, beauty and charm, are among the most engaging of all garden creatures. Attracting them is a matter of offering nectar-rich flowers for the adults and foliage for the caterpillars.

Water elements provide moisture and pleasing accents, although butterflies will be happy with just a damp spot of earth.

Flowers, the primary source of nectar for butterflies, give the garden color and charm.

Trees offer protection from the sun and wind and host the eggs and caterpillars of many butterfly species.

Shrubs help give the garden landscape form and provide food and shelter for many butterflies.

GARDEN ELEMENTS

The first step in creating a garden that attracts butterflies is to observe which species live nearby. Look in gardens, parks, vacant lots and open spaces on warm, still mornings or afternoons when butterflies are most active. Use field guides to identify individual species and the plants they're attracted to.

Then select a sunny area protected from the wind and predators. Incorporate as many plants as you can to attract the most butterflies. A combination of cultivated and native plants including wildflowers is most effective. Butterflies are attracted to trees, shrubs, ground covers, grasses, vines and many garden flowers. They thrive in environments free of pesticides and herbicides.

Nectar from flowers is essential for adult butterflies (see pages 28–29). In general, they prefer colorful, fragrant flowers with surfaces large enough to land on.

Foliage to feed hungry caterpillars is also important. Numerous trees, shrubs, herbs and grasses meet this need (see pages 34–35). The walls and windbreaks formed by shrubs or trees help shelter butterflies as do meadow areas if grasses are allowed to grow tall.

Water elements, whether they are formal fountains, small ponds or muddy puddles, are also important. Besides providing moisture for butterflies, they become refreshing focal points in the garden.

Like birds, butterflies come to rely on the food and shelter you offer. With a minimum of effort, your garden will become more than a pleasing, diverse landscape. It will evolve into an environment where plants and animals—including butterflies—thrive.

LIFE CYCLE OF THE BUTTERFLY

Part of what makes butterflies so intriguing is the incredible series of changes that takes them to adulthood. Eggs laid on leaves by adult butterflies hatch into caterpillars that feed constantly and then encase themselves in delicate chambers to emerge in a matter of weeks as beautiful, graceful butterflies. Amazing!

The life cycle, beginning with an adult butterfly such as this mourning cloak perched on a willow leaf, can progress from egg to larva to adult in only a few weeks. The life span for most butterflies is only two weeks, though some live six to eight months.

Developmental Stages

First After mating, the adult female selects just the right plant to lay her eggs on. A mourning cloak butterfly has deposited her tiny eggs on the stem. Butterflies lay from two or three to several hundred eggs, most hatching within a week, some lasting over winter or up to two years. A strong membrane covers the egg, which is usually of the same color as the adult butterfly.

Third The caterpillar finishes growing and finds a protected spot to form the chrysalis. After spinning a silken pad and hooking its end pair of legs, the caterpillar molts into a chrysalis, which may hang upside down or right side up. Inside the chrysalis, phenomenal changes take place. The caterpillar's body tissues break down as it begins transforming into a butterfly. After about five days tiny wings are visible.

Then Caterpillars are veritable eating machines with specialized mouth parts for chewing and several pairs of jointed, clawed legs for locomotion. Internally, caterpillars are similar to butterflies but with more highly developed glands. As the caterpillar grows, it sheds its rigid outer skin several times. Many caterpillars are camouflaged in varying shades of green, while others have colorful markings or spines to deter predators. Some caterpillars overwinter in this stage if conditions are not right for surviving in a chrysalis or in adult form.

Last In 10–14 days for most species (some chrysalises last through winter), the adult butterfly is ready to hatch. Usually with the help of the warm morning sun, the butterfly emerges with a swollen body. As fluids are pumped into the unfolding wings, the body shrinks. In an hour or so the butterfly is ready for flight and begins the courtship and mating ritual right away. In warm climates several generations live and die each year. Fewer broods are produced in areas where cold weather either kills adults or forces longer-lived species into hibernation.

NECTAR-RICH FLOWERS

A LIQUID FEAST

Nectar, the sweet liquid inside a flower, is an adult butterfly's main source of nourishment. Simple flowers with tubular shapes or those with clusters of tubular florets are usually a good source for nectar, especially when rimmed with a flat surface for perching. Butterflies are attracted to flowers by color and scent. They seem to prefer bright colors such as red, orange and yellow, but they also visit purple, lavender and blue flowers. Just about any scented flower with nectar and an open, accessible petal arrangement will attract them. Many good butterfly flowers come from the daisy family, which includes asters, goldenrods, dahlias, marigolds and zinnias.

Wildflowers are another prime source of nectar for butterflies. Butterfly weed, ironweed, coneflower (rudbeckia), thistles, vetches, wild yarrow and even dogbane and milkweed are all meadow plants that successfully attract butterflies. Some of these integrate beautifully into the garden. Others can be grown in "wild" unused areas of the yard and will attract many species, including skippers, admirals, ladies and monarchs.

The flower garden need not be large, as long as it has a variety of plants with a succession of flowers. Choose several plants to bloom from summer into fall, if conditions permit. Plant drifts or masses, fill window boxes or patio containers, create mounds with flowers spilling down the slopes, or install traditional flower beds alongside walkways and lawns.

Annuals

Ageratum, *Ageratum houstonianum*, is a bright edging or container plant covered with clusters of tiny blue, purple or pink flowers summer through fall. It takes sun to part shade.

Dianthus, also called pinks, *Dianthus chinensis*, has a sweet fragrance that makes it perfect in beds, borders or containers. It takes sun to partial shade and good to poor soil.

Lobelia, *Lobelia erinus*, is nearly covered by delicate but profuse violet, blue, pink or white flowers. Its trailing habit makes it effective as an edging, container or low border plant.

Sweet alyssum, *Lobularia maritima,* with clusters of fragrant flowers in white, rose, pink, apricot or violet is easily grown from seed. It's good for borders, among bulbs and in containers.

Flowering tobacco, *Nicotiana* species, has been a longtime favorite for its bold, fragrant tubular flowers. It grows 2–4 ft. tall with striking red, pink, purple, white or lavender flowers in summer.

Verbena, *Verbena* x *hybrida,* offers an almost unparalleled summer display of flowers in many colors. This plant takes sun, tolerates heat and works nicely in baskets and containers.

Perennials

Butterfly weed, *Asclepias tuberosa,* produces clusters of fragrant yellow-orange flowers that butterflies love. It blooms well in sun and tolerates many soils if it has good drainage.

Purple coneflower, *Echinacea purpurea*, has daisy-like flowers with dark centers. Purple, white, pink or red flowers last from summer into fall. The light fragrance attracts butterflies.

Wallflower, *Erysimum linifolium,* blooms from spring through fall producing long spikes with clusters of lavender to purple flowers. 'Variegatum' has narrow leaves edged in white.

Sea pink, *Armeria* species, is an excellent small-space ground cover with dense mounds of grassy foliage and ball-like clusters of white, pink, rose or red flowers.

Shasta daisy, *Chrysanthemum* x *superbum,* with classic white-and-yellow flowers and dark green foliage, is a good choice for beds, borders, mass plantings and cutting gardens.

Candytuft, *Iberis sempervirens,* has dark green foliage that is covered with white flowers in spring. Use it in rock gardens, containers and borders. It needs trimming after it blooms.

SHRUBS FOR BUTTERFLIES

FOOD & MORE

Shrubs are an important part of a landscape that attracts butterflies. Their leaves and branches house eggs, feed caterpillars and offer hiding and warming stations. Those that flower often provide nectar for adults.

To provide nectar, choose several varieties of flowering shrubs with long bloom times so that butterflies will have a continuous source of food. Select shrubs that complement annuals and perennials or that flower when other plants do not. Plant scented varieties near walkways, or patios and under windows. Planting shrubs in groups makes for impressive displays; changing height and texture keeps the garden visually interesting.

If space is limited, try a butterfly bush, *Buddleia* species. This shrub draws many common backyard butterflies with its multiple clusters of flowers with honey-like fragrance. Even a single plant will attract several butterfly species.

If you have a small garden or need to fill in among larger shrubs and trees, look for compact or low-growing shrubs and ground covers. Sometimes shrubs in the same family will range from low, spreading plants to tall specimens, as is the case with colorful spiraea or weigela.

Shelter for butterflies is easy to provide. Dense shrubbery of almost any kind will offer open places for warming wings or concealed spots for hiding from birds, lizards or cats. Often, the same shrubs that provide nectar for butterflies or leaves for caterpillars also offer excellent shelter. A small woodpile with a canvas or tarp covering over just the top is an excellent shelter for roosting or hibernating butterflies.

Common butterfly bush, *Buddleia davidii*, rates number one for attracting butterflies because of its many fragrant flower clusters on arching branch tips. This showy, vigorous grower reaches 5–10 ft. and offers a wide range of summer flowers in lilac, purple, pink, reddish purple or white. In cold climates, cut the bush back almost to the ground each spring; in mild regions prune in the fall after flowers fade. Use this shrub for background plantings, informal hedges or colorful accents. It attracts many species, including monarchs, whites, painted ladies and swallowtails.

Fountain butterfly bush, *Buddleia alternifolia*, offers sweetly scented lilac to light purple flowers in spring. Graceful, arching stems tipped with flower clusters give it an airy, delicate look, although it can reach 12 ft. Like all buddleias, this shrub takes full sun to light shade and occasional to regular water. Blossoms form on old wood, so prune after flowering to promote new growth for the following year's display. Use in mass plantings, as a background shrub or to fill in between other shrubs. It attracts skippers, red admirals, commas, mourning cloaks and many other butterflies.

Bumalda spiraea, *Spiraea* x *bumalda* 'Golden flame', with tiny white, pink or red flowers on slender arching stems, is a valuable garden addition. These deciduous plants are easy to grow and range 2–4 ft. tall. With a light, airy texture and pretty fall color, they're useful as accent plants, massed plantings and informal screens. They prefer regular watering and full sun but tolerate some shade and a variety of soils. Japanese spiraea, *S. japonica,* is more upright and grows to 6 ft. Spiraeas attract skippers, cabbage whites and other butterflies.

Lilac, *Syringa vulgaris,* shown here in May, has long been prized for its fragrant beauty. These deciduous shrubs reach 10–20 ft. and offer clusters of purple, lavender, white, pink or red flowers. Lilacs are long-lived and easy to care for, preferring full sun and average soil and watering. Use them as informal screens, background plants or accents and for cut flowers. Remove spent flowers and shape young plants by pinching the soft new growth. These shrubs attract many butterfly species, including hairstreaks, swallowtails and mourning cloaks.

Lantanas produce lavender, yellow, red, pink, orange or multicolor flowers nearly nonstop from spring until frost. Shrubs range from upright 4–6 ft. *Lantana camara,* shown here in summer, to the trailing *Lantana montevidensis.* Use trailing varieties in containers or for ground cover and erosion control. Shrubs can be used as foundation plants, low hedges or accents. These easy-care plants are sun loving and tolerate heat, poor soil and drought. Lantanas prefer mild winters but can be grown as annuals or perennials in cold climates. They attract skippers, swallowtails, cabbage whites and others.

Beautybush, *Kolkwitzia amabilis,* shown here, is prized for its display of cascading clusters of yellow-throated pink blooms in May–June. Distinctive pink-brown, bristled fruits form after flowering and add interest to the garden throughout the summer. Beautybush reaches 12 ft. Use as a hedging or accent plant. It provides nectar and shelter for hummingbirds.

TREES & GRASSES FOR BUTTERFLIES

ADDITIONAL FOOD & SHELTER SOURCES

Trees and grasses are important sources of food and shelter for butterflies.

Trees provide food in several forms. In spring, nectar from flowering trees is enjoyed by swallowtails and others. Later in the season rotting fruit is an important part of the diet for many butterflies, including the comma, mourning cloak and viceroy. Some butterflies, such as satyrs, admirals and question marks, rely on running tree sap for nourishment. Voracious caterpillars eat tree leaves. On just one tree, adults may drink nectar, feed on sap and lay eggs on leaves that are later eaten by the caterpillars. Silver birch, redtwig dogwood, English hawthorn, poplar, willow, elm and alder are trees that provide food for both adults and larvae.

Butterflies also need trees for perching, sunning and hiding from predators. Dense trees, such as pine, spruce and cedar, offer safe harbors in cold, hot or windy conditions and at night when butterflies roost. They also provide camouflage for many species.

As you plan for trees in the garden, remember that sunlight is critical for butterflies, because without warmth they cannot fly. Place tall nectar-producing plants and sheltering trees on the perimeter of open areas for the best exposure.

Some butterflies, including most of the skippers and many satyrs, lay their eggs on grasses, which support the caterpillars. Ornamental and native grasses provide shelter at different heights and perches for sunning. In the garden, they offer natural accents and soft contrast to broadleaf shrubs and trees.

Trees

Willows, such as this summer weeping willow, *Salix babylonica*, are fast-growing, adaptable trees. Willows attract mourning cloaks, swallowtails, viceroys and admirals.

Grasses

Stipa or Mexican feathergrass, *Stipa tenuissima*, is useful among shrubs, as an accent or in naturalized gardens. It serves well alone or in groups and mixed with perennials. It hosts skippers, satyrs and others.

Chinese elm, *Ulmus parvifolia,* is easy to grow in many conditions including heat, drought and poor or compacted soil. It draws mourning cloaks and commas.

Flowering dogwood, *Cornus florida,* has a beautiful show of flowers in the spring. Butterflies find shelter amid its leaves and branches and some use it for egg laying.

Quaking grass, *Briza media*, is a perennial grass with graceful, nodding clusters of heart-shaped seed heads that dangle on slim stems and tremble in the breeze. Clumps attract skippers and others.

Moor grass, *Molinia caerulea*, also known as Indian grass, offers feathery green leaves and purplish branching stems of multiple flower clusters in late summer and fall. It attracts skippers, nymphs and others.

FEEDING CATERPILLARS

LARVAL FOOD

With the right plants, you can encourage butterflies to lay their eggs in the garden and then watch as hatched caterpillars transform into beautiful butterflies. If you're willing to share your plants with them, you can expect your sacrifice to be small; the damage caused by caterpillars is usually temporary.

Many trees, flowers, herbs and vegetables make good larval food plants. Native wildflowers host many butterfly species, including monarchs, who feed on milkweed and dogbane. If you have space to let part of the yard go "wild," try clover, vetch, thistle, sweet pea, dock, nettle and grasses. These plants host many species that rely on such low-maintenance perennials for food and shelter. Scatter seeds or simply let volunteers take over in an out-of-the-way patch, and you'll have a wonderful haven for caterpillars.

Another option is to plant deciduous trees, which are favored by many species. Willow, elm, ash, hackberry, hawthorn, cottonwood, poplar and fruit trees are excellent. Several species of oak attract hairstreak, skipper and duskywing butterflies. Decide what you want from a landscape standpoint—shade, fruit, fall color, shape, size—and find larval food trees with these features.

Shrubs, perennials or vegetables also serve as larval food. Viburnums, lilacs, mallows and cinquefoil are excellent shrubs. Asters are versatile, colorful perennials that support brightly patterned checkerspot and crescentspot butterflies and their larvae. Rock cress, *Arabis* species, hosts several species, as do violets. You'll attract swallowtails and others with a planting of carrots, parsley and dill.

As host to cabbage butterflies, nasturtiums are easy-to-grow annuals that bloom in summer and fall with bright yellow, red, orange, white or pink flowers.

Host Plants

Trees such as this hawthorne, *Crataegus* species, fill a variety of landscape needs and feed larvae at the same time. Hawthornes offer beautiful clusters of flowers in the spring, followed by colorful fruits in the summer and fall. Growing to 25 ft., they host white admiral, red-spotted purple and grey hairstreak butterflies.

Flowers, such as this hollyhock, *Alcea rosea,* are often excellent hosts for caterpillars. Painted ladies and common checkered skippers lay eggs on hollyhocks, which provide tall accents and rich color in the flower border. These perennials reach up to 8 ft. with spires of large flowers in every shade except blue. Violets, which are perennials, host several species of fritillary butterflies. Their low mounds of attractive foliage and fragrant spring flowers are perfect for mixed beds and borders.

Shrubs help define a garden's layout and often provide food for hungry caterpillars. Cinquefoils, *Potentilla* species, shown here, have glossy strawberry-like leaves and bright rose-like flowers in yellow, pink, red or white. These shrubs range 1–5 ft. in height and bloom from June until frost in sunny spots. They tolerate drought, poor soil and heat and attract copper butterflies. Junipers also host caterpillars and work well as evergreen foundation and background plants. Check with field guides for native shrubs that may attract local species.

Grasses make up a broad category of host plants that feed many species of satyr and skipper butterflies. This St. Augustine grass, *Stenotaphrum secundatum,* is a tough, broad-bladed lawn grass that stands up well to intense use. Limited to the southern states and the Southwest, it withstands heat and does best with frequent watering. Use ornamental grasses, including fescues, *Festuca* species, and moor grass, *Molinia caerulea,* for texture, in rock and natural gardens and with other perennials.

GARDEN DESIGN

DESIGN CONSIDERATIONS

The key to a successful garden is a well thought-out design that makes the most of the site while meeting the goals of the gardener. An artistic design comes from effectively using the principles of form, scale, rhythm, color and texture.

Begin by searching for ideas in books and magazines or by visiting public gardens and the yards of friends and neighbors. Set a preliminary budget and make a list of important elements and goals you have for the garden. Include rough cost estimates.

Decide what form or shape the garden will have. In a garden that attracts wildlife, leaf cleanup, shrub trimming and other general maintenance is kept to a minimum. An informal garden with free-form beds and flowing lines may be more appropriate than a formal garden, where straight lines and symmetrical elements seem to demand a more manicured approach.

Choose a design that fits the scale of the space and fits into the surrounding area. Repeat shapes, materials or plant groupings to unify the garden and create a pleasing rhythm. Combine leaf textures that go well together, or select individual plants with interesting textures to highlight specific areas. Accent with focal points such as a pond, birdbath or specimen plant.

Let color add character and mood to the garden. Choose cool blues and greens to make spaces appear larger and more restful. Accent with warm reds, oranges and yellows—energetic colors that pop out and attract attention. Experiment with contrasting colors such as yellow and purple or harmonious colors like yellow and orange. Consider foliage color and seasonal changes, too.

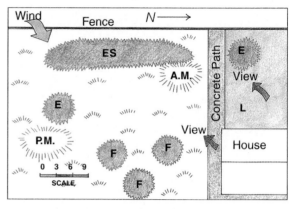

Successful Planning

First   Drawing the Base Plan
A.M. = morning sun; **P.M.** = afternoon sun;
E = evergreen tree; **ES** = evergreen shrubs;
F = fruit tree; **L** = lawn

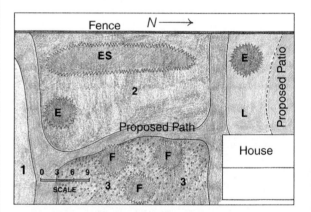

Then   Choosing the Site
E = evergreen tree; **ES** = evergreen shrubs;
F = fruit tree; **L** = lawn;
1 = proposed heirloom perennial garden;
2 = proposed bird and butterfly garden site;
3 = bark

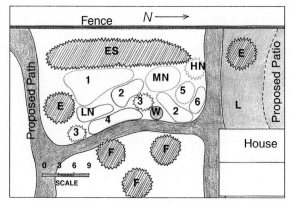

Third Preparing the Bubble Diagrams

LN = low nesting source; **MN** = medium nesting source; **HN** = high nesting source; **W** = water element; **1** = flowers for butterflies; **2** = flowers for birds; **3** = fruit source; **4** = seed source; **5** = nectar source; **6** = berry source

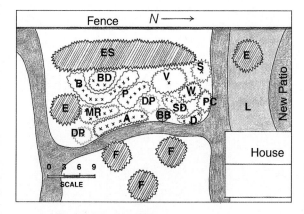

Last Finalizing the Plan

A = annuals for seeds; **B** = buddleia; **BB** = birdbath; **BD** = buddleia davidii; **D** = dianthus; **DP** = dwarf peach; **MR** = mini-rose; **P** = penstemon; **PC** = pyracantha; **S** = spruce; **SD** = shasta daisy; **V** = viburnum; **W** = wallflower

DRAWING SIMPLE PLANS

Having a plan on paper helps you visualize the garden and prepare for installation. You'll need a measuring tape, graph paper, tracing paper, ruler, colored pencils, eraser, straight edge or T-square and templates (or a good hand) to draw curves and circles. Each square on graph paper represents one foot in the garden. Pick a scale that best fits the dimensions of your garden. The sample drawings at left use a scale of nine feet per inch.

Drawing the Base Plan

Measure your garden and fill in the basic shapes and dimensions on a base plan. Include all fixed elements such as the house, fence, patios and paths plus all plants you hope to retain. Evaluate your site and indicate exposures to wind, sun and views you hope to keep or block.

Choosing the Site

Spend time outside and with the base plan determining the exact location in your yard best suited to a bird and butterfly garden. At the same time, create a wish list of the plants and other elements you most want to feature in your specialty garden.

Preparing the Bubble Diagram

Broadly outline—on a photocopy of your base plan (or on tracing paper)—elements from your wish list. Experiment until you're satisfied. Keep in mind the site limitations, access, maintenance needs and the general types of plants and features for the animals you hope to attract.

Finalizing the Plan

Finalize the plan by neatly drawing each element to scale and filling in specific plants. Consider plant height and spread when determining where and how many plants to install. Use this plan to make shopping lists and when installing garden elements. The real garden based on the plan at left is shown on pages 38-39.

A SAMPLE GARDEN

Successful garden designs transform ordinary areas into special places that highlight the best nature has to offer. Gardens that attract birds and butterflies are examples of how various elements can be combined into beautiful settings that benefit wildlife. Ultimately the result is great enjoyment for all who share the garden.

Focal points, like this butterfly bush, add definition to the garden and invite the attention of visitors.

Water—cooling, refreshing and relaxing—gives the garden character and meets an essential need for wildlife.

Vines add vertical interest and provide quick greenery for fences, walls and trellises.

Trees and shrubs, both permanent and prominent elements, should be chosen and planted first, because it may take them several years to reach their full size.

Seating elements allow us to linger in the garden where we can enjoy the spectacle of life that nature offers.

Pathways encourage the use of the whole garden and provide access for maintenance.

Flowers draw us—and other creatures—into the garden with their enchanting colors, fragrances and nectar.

IMPROVING THE SOIL

Nothing is more important to the garden than a healthy, living soil. Whether you have dense clay, fine silt or coarse sand, the right amendments—such as the compost being worked into the soil here—can help ensure success. The combination of well-prepared soil and plants suited to that soil leads to beautiful, thriving gardens.

Spread a 2–4 in. layer of compost and work it into the top several inches of the soil, where roots need it most.

BENEFITS OF COMPOST

Most garden soils improve greatly with the addition of simple amendments such as compost. Compost is partially decomposed organic material. It is dark, crumbly and rich in nutrients.

In heavy or clay soils, compost helps break up dense particles and improve structure and drainage. In loose, fast-draining sandy soils, compost helps increase moisture retention and gives the soil a better structure. Because good compost is rich in nitrogen, phosphorus and potassium as well as trace nutrients, it boosts soil fertility.

Compost is formed when microorganisms break down raw organic materials that are gathered together in a pile or a simple enclosure. These organisms, and other creatures such as earthworms, digest the raw materials and leave behind a decayed finished product.

Garden waste (leaves, grass, spent blossoms, pine needles), kitchen scraps (other than meat and fat), straw, hay, wood ashes and barnyard manures compost well; however, manure that has not aged can harm plants. Avoid twigs larger than pencil size because they take too long to decay.

A simple wire or wooden enclosure that keeps out animals is perfect for a compost pile. Start with a two-inch layer of loosely piled leaves, hay or grass clippings. Sprinkle on a thin layer of nitrogen fertilizer and a layer of well-rotted manure. Then add a layer of good garden soil, which supplies the organisms. Repeat these layers several times. Sprinkle the pile with water to keep it moist. If it becomes dry, the decaying process will stop. Turn the pile weekly for good air circulation. Within several weeks to a few months, the compost will be ready.

You may find birds attracted to the pile looking for exposed seeds or worms. Butterflies may visit too in search of moisture, rotting fruit or other nectar sources.

INSTALLING PLANTS

PLANT SELECTION

When it comes to plants for the bird and butterfly garden, you can either start seeds or buy transplants in containers at garden centers and nurseries.

Annual and perennial flowers can be started from seeds or transplanted from small packs or four-inch pots. Seeds offer great variety, economy (they cost far less than container plants) and satisfaction as you watch them grow into beautiful blooming plants. Transplants give your garden a head start.

Seed packets tell you when to start seeds indoors or out, and how and where to use the plants in the garden. Indoors, give the plants plenty of light (but not direct sun) near bright windows or under fluorescent plant lights. When they're about ready to plant *harden* them by putting them outside for increasing periods of time each day for a week or so.

Transplanting from containers is practical for trees, shrubs, ground covers and other large plants. Select plants in 1-, 5- or 15-gallon containers for the most immediate impact; keep in mind that larger plants are harder to install and may take longer to get established. Choosing plants in the season they bloom or bear fruit allows you to preview their performance in the garden.

Select healthy container plants by inspecting the foliage and roots. The leaves should show new growth and have good color. They should be well formed, of normal size and free of pests and diseases. Tangled roots growing out of the bottom of the container indicate that the plant is probably rootbound and should be avoided.

Starting Seed Indoors

First Purchase fresh seeds suitable for your region. Fill a clean, flat container with sterilized potting soil and soak the soil thoroughly.

Then Sow the seeds. Sow more seeds than you think you'll need; later, choose the healthiest seedlings. Firm the soil by tamping it down lightly with your fingers.

Third Use a spray bottle to water the soil gently; water should be at room temperature. Take care not to overwater or let the container sit in water.

Fourth Clearly label plants and cover them with plastic wrap to keep moisture in. It's critical to keep the soil moist so the sprouting seeds and seedlings do not dry out.

Next Put the container in a warm, bright location or under a household fluorescent bulb 18 hours per day until seeds sprout. If you use fluorescent lights, raise the lights as the seedlings grow.

Last Remove the plastic when seeds sprout. Keep the soil moist. Transplant seedlings when they have two or three sets of true leaves. True leaves follow the first rounded leaves that emerge at sprouting time.

First Dig a hole the same depth and twice as wide as the rootball. Roughen and loosen the soil on the sides and bottom with a spading fork. Mix in a slow-release fertilizer.

Next Moisten the rootball and slide the plant out sideways. Cut circling roots; loosen others. Set the plant in the hole so that the soil at the base of the trunk is at ground level.

Last Fill around the plant with amended soil firming around the roots. Water regularly and deeply for the first year. Stake trees outside the rootball.

Maintaining the Garden

The Natural Look

Maintenance in a garden that attracts birds and butterflies is different from in other gardens. Chemicals that harm birds and butterflies are avoided and leaving plant debris at times is acceptable. Such an environment often has a more "wild" appeal than a perfectly groomed landscape. Although the goal is still to keep the garden looking its best, the approach must be one of patience and tolerance.

In some cases, maintenance tasks must be delayed. Allowing plants to go to seed, rather than clipping every spent blossom, provides valuable food for many birds and may give you volunteer seedlings later on. Letting plants bloom until every bud opens, instead of trimming to avoid legginess, provides nectar for the hummingbirds and butterflies.

Basic, ongoing maintenance tasks help keep plants vigorous and enable them to tolerate damage from pests and diseases. Watering depends on your soil type and climate. Do not let your plants get to the wilting stage before watering them.

Fertilizing helps make nutrients available for plants to grow vigorously. Mix granular or timed-release pellets into the top layer of the soil to provide plants with a steady supply of nutrients. Natural fertilizers such as bone meal, fish emulsion, crushed oyster shells and well-rotted manure spread around the base of plants are effective organic alternatives to chemical fertilizers.

Mulching keeps soil moist and helps control weeds, which can be pulled easily while still small. Pruning removes damaged or diseased wood and promotes growth.

Maintenance Tasks

Watering at the base of the plant with a slow trickle prevents run-off. Drip irrigation is a convenient alternative that uses tubing and emitters to deliver water directly to plants. Occasionally wash the dust off leaves—early in the day so that foliage has time to dry off.

Mulching helps retain soil moisture and keeps weeds down. Mulches such as compost, leaves or grass clippings provide organic materials for the soil. Spread 2–3 in. of mulch around the base of the plant, keeping it several inches from the trunk.

Weeding is easiest when weeds are small. If you can tolerate them, allow a patch to grow in an out-of-the-way spot to provide flowers for butterflies, seeds for birds and leaves for caterpillars.

Grooming keeps the garden tidy and helps discourage diseases and pests. Trim spent blossoms and stems from plants that do not produce desirable seeds. Others should be left to dry and spill seeds for birds.

Fertilizing regularly during periods of active growth allows plants to grow well and produce flowers, seeds and foliage for food. Applying organic fertilizers such as this liquid fish emulsion is a safe, natural method.

Pruning keeps plants producing at peak levels. Cut out broken, diseased or crossing branches. Trim fruit trees, flowering shrubs, berry bushes and perennials to increase flower and fruit production. Leave the occasional tree stump as a nesting site and insect source.

SEASONAL CARE

SPRING, SUMMER & FALL CARE

Each season brings change to the bird and butterfly garden. As the first spring buds open, migrating birds and emerging butterflies return to the garden. Fruit trees and flowering shrubs become clouds of color and provide small buds and insects for finches and others. Sap begins flowing from holes made by woodpeckers; hummingbirds and others feast on the sugary food and the insects attracted to it. Some plants produce fruit. This is a good time to phase out winter feeders to keep birds from dependency.

In spring, gardening activites are centered around planting. Set out fresh annuals and perennials, and plant shrubs and trees when cold weather is over. Enjoy cut sprays of flowering shrubs, most of which are best pruned during or after they bloom.

Summer in the garden brings flowers, fruit and heightened activity from many garden visitors. Nesting season is in full swing and youngsters call loudly to their parents for meals. Birds need plenty of water and shade in the summer. The season accelerates the life cycle of many butterflies, so besides more butterflies you may notice more chewed leaves from caterpillars. Watering, weeding and fertilizing plants in active growth are part of the summer gardening routine.

In fall many birds gather into flocks, and begin to migrate. Butterfly numbers decline as cold weather sets in. Flowers begin to fade as autumn color and bountiful berries appear. Fall is a good time to complete garden cleanup and plant spring bulbs. In mild climates, you can plant all but the most tender plants in the fall.

Good winter care results in an active spring garden filled with budding trees, blooming flowers and nesting birds.

WINTER CARE

Winter in the garden is a time of quiet beauty as the garden takes on a new look and cold weather dictates special garden activities.

Winter protection may be necessary for some plants if you live in a cold region. Roses and many perennials benefit from a 6–12 inch layer of mulch. Gradually remove the covering in spring.

Winter is the season for pruning dormant fruit trees and many flowering deciduous plants. Thin out overgrown plants and shape others for optimum form. Remove damaged, diseased and crossing branches.

In warmer climates, set out annuals such as primroses, pansies, stock, calendula and snapdragons for winter and early spring blooms, that, on warm days, may be visited by hummingbirds or butterflies.

As the season gets cooler, many birds will disappear, preferring warmer locations. Those that remain—including cardinals, jays, northern flickers, mourning doves, sparrows, purple finches, chickadees, titmice and many woodpeckers—concentrate on feeding. You can help by maintaining well-stocked feeding stations (see pages 58–59).

Providing water is helpful but not essential during cold, freezing weather. Birds can usually obtain enough drinking water from snow, but they may not be able to find bathing water. You can keep the water in birdbaths from freezing by installing special, commercially available heaters made for the purpose.

Butterflies cope with winter in a number of ways. Hairstreaks and swallowtails overwinter as eggs. Viceroy and white admiral caterpillars roll up in leaves, and adult mourning cloaks, tortoiseshells and angelwings hibernate in tree hollows or buildings. Other butterflies simply die off in the coldest portions of their range and are replaced by offspring that have overwintered or by butterflies that migrated to the warmer part of the range and return in the spring.

A FEW CHEWED LEAVES

In a garden environment set up to attract wildlife the number one rule is: Use No Pesticides, especially if you're attracting butterflies. Caterpillars and many beneficial insects will suffer.

There *are* safe methods of control. The first line of defense is to grow strong plants. Place plants where they have optimum growing conditions. Proper soil preparation, fertilization and irrigation will help plants defend themselves.

Tolerance is another key. Gardens are miniature ecological environments and pests are part of the package. They usually cause no severe damage.

To minimize damage, there are several options. Hand picking or trapping is practical for snails, slugs and earwigs. Set out inverted pots or old pieces of hose, which serve as hiding places. In the morning, search for the pests concealed there.

Birds in the garden help control many insects, including aphids. But if aphids are causing damage, shoot them with a spray from the hose or with a weak solution of soapy water followed by clear water.

Some pests flourish in decaying leaves and plant material. Clean up debris, but remember that twigs and mosses are valuable during nest-building season.

Lastly, encourage beneficial insects such as ladybird beetles, which feed on aphids and scale insects, and assassin bugs and praying mantises, which feed on a variety of pests. You can buy beneficial insects from some nurseries and mail-order companies. Release them at night so they will begin feeding when they awake in the morning.

Most of this plant has been left intact in spite of some pest damage, possibly caused by feeding caterpillars.

RESISTING DISEASE

A garden with diseased plants cannot live up to its potential. Avoiding disease, rather than rescuing sick plants, is the key to success.

Preventing disease helps eliminate the need for chemicals, which can harm birds and butterflies as well as humans. Give plants proper growing conditions for peak performance and maintain a sanitary environment. Perhaps even more important is to choose disease-resistant varieties.

Many of the plants cultivated for home landscapes have been developed to be tough and to resist diseases. Likewise, many old-fashioned favorites preferred by birds and butterflies have survived for centuries because of their natural disease resistance. You'll be getting your garden off to a good start by selecting varieties noted for disease resistance. This is especially true for fruit trees, so check varieties for this feature.

Plants that have been placed in the wrong location in the garden are often more susceptible to disease. A plant that likes dry to slightly moist soil will languish in a spot that stays waterlogged. Crowded plants won't have adequate air circulation and may become diseased. Those that like sun will be weakened if grown in a location with too much shade.

Sanitation goes a long way in keeping diseases in check. Inspect for and remove discolored, disfigured and rotted leaves, flowers, stems and branches. Look on leaf undersides for signs of distress and disease. This is especially important with fungal diseases such as powdery mildew, character-ized by silver powdery patches on leaves and flowers. Leaf spot, rust and peach leaf curl are other examples of fungal diseases. Espe-cially in winter, collect, bag and discard all damaged leaves to keep these diseases from recurring. Do not place diseased leaves in the compost pile.

WATER IN THE GARDEN

AN ESSENTIAL ELEMENT

One of the most important features of a wild-life garden is water. Besides attracting birds and butterflies, water helps create a focal point and set the mood for the landscape.

Birds will benefit most from water elements. They're attracted to water for drinking and bathing and accept water in many forms. Be sure to keep the water clean, and never allow chemicals to get into the water.

A small backyard pond (see pages 52–53) with water plants and fish will delight all of your garden guests. No matter how small your pond, make safety a key consideration. Secure fences and gates are a must.

Be aware that the pond may draw less desirable wildlife, including raccoons and birds such as kingfishers. These animals, which are difficult to control, will go after fish, frogs and other pond creatures.

As attractive as a pond may be, birds really don't require anything so elaborate. They'll welcome moisture from the sprinkler or gravitate to sunken tubs or saucers. Just about any container with sloping edges will work, although most birds prefer those that are shallow—no more than two to three inches deep.

Supplying water for butterflies is very simple. Besides collecting moisture from morning dew, butterflies, often in large numbers, are attracted to puddles or damp areas.

Locate different water elements throughout the yard to ensure a variety of garden visitors. Some birds like water set out in an open area, while others prefer water placed near protective cover. Many perch on a nearby tree, then drop down for a drink or a bath when they know it is safe.

Water elements can be quite simple, yet expressive sources of moisture, as this hollowed stone illustrates.

Water Sources

Fountains make excellent water elements for birds because they provide water for drinking and a spray for bathing. They also serve as attractive accents.

Birdbaths should be 3 ft. off the ground and in the open. A basin with a diameter of 24–36 in. will attract a community of bathers; anything smaller will serve 1 or 2 birds at a time.

Shallow saucers are simple and effective water sources. Rather than leave a faucet dripping, fill a bucket, pierce a small hole in the side and suspend it above the container.

CREATING A BACKYARD POND

A small backyard pond is easy to install if you use a shallow, preformed pool. Filled with fish and aquatic plants, it will add an appealing focal point to your garden as well as attract birds and butterflies.

This preformed pool has been lined with rocks and stocked with aquatic plants and fish.

Installing a Water Garden

First Select a site that you'll be able to enjoy from indoors or nearby seating areas. The site should receive full sun and attract a minimum of leaf litter.

Then Choose a strong and durable pool made of fiberglass, semi-rigid ABS plastic or bonded resin. More flexible shells need complete support so they don't sag or crack when filled.

Third Dig a basin 2 in. wider and deeper than the shell to allow for a layer of sand. A garden hose can be used to outline the area to be dug. Level the bottom of the basin, then add 2 in. of sand. Level the bottom again.

Fourth Lower the shell, making sure it rests evenly on the sand. Slowly fill the shell with water; as the shell settles, backfill along the sides with sand or soil, tamping firmly.

Fifth Place rocks around the pool rim, forming an overhang of 2 in. to hide the edges. Vary the size of the rocks for a natural look. Large, flat rocks make good perches for birds.

Sixth Install a submersible pump to create waterfalls or fountains. Use special outdoor cord connected to a professionally installed electrical outlet. Clean the pump's filter screen on a regular basis.

Seventh Include a variety of plants for a visually and ecologically balanced pool. Place baskets or wide plastic pots at different depths depending on plant requirements.

Next Plant aquatic or bog plants in a heavy garden soil that has no pesticide or herbicide residue. Many beautiful flowering plants can be submerged or left to float on the surface.

Last Add fish after the water has cured for at least 24 hours. Use dechlorinating drops initially and each time you add water. Float the fish in sealed water-filled bags for 15 minutes before releasing them.

Building a Birdhouse

This wooden house is designed for a titmouse and should be mounted 6–15 feet above the ground on a post, pole or tree trunk away from predators and noise.

Helping Nature

Birdhouses or nest boxes placed in the garden in late winter attract breeding pairs who normally nest in natural cavities such as rock crevices or tree hollows. The best material for nest boxes and birdhouses is rot-resistant wood such as redwood or cedar.

The size and style of the birdhouse will dictate what bird nests there. Do not build an "all-purpose" birdhouse to attract a variety of species. These usually do not work. Determine which birds you're likely to attract, and consult a chart for the dimensions of the house and the diameter and height of the entrance hole those species require. Wrens, chickadees, titmice, swallows, house sparrows and flickers are easy to attract.

Some species, including robins, barn swallows, song sparrows and phoebes prefer nesting platforms with one or more sides open. These houses feature a high roof and a platform with half-inch-high sides.

Most birds, except wrens, will not use a hanging birdhouse because it jiggles and sways in the wind. They prefer a box securely fastened to a tree trunk, wooden post or metal pipe. Place the birdhouse 6–15 feet above the ground, depending on the species. Locate the box so that the entrance faces away from prevailing winds, and tilt it slightly downward to keep out rain.

Keep squirrels, chipmunks and cats from getting to a hanging birdhouse by placing the box away from side branches. For houses mounted on a pole or post, attach a cone-shaped sheet metal collar under the box to discourage climbers.

Inviting Long-term Guests

First Determine the dimensions required by the bird species you want to attract. Use ¾ in. wood. The back panel should be larger than all the other pieces. Clamp the side pieces together and cut them, angling the top. Cut the front with a slightly beveled edge, and construct the floor to fit between the sides. Size the roof to create an overhang of 1½ in. all around.

Third Join the sides to the bottom using galvanized nails, nails and waterproof glue, or brass screws. Nails hold the pieces in place while the glue, which is a good sealant, dries. (For wood that splits easily, predrill nail holes slightly smaller than the nail.) Allowing room at the top for the roof, center these joined pieces on the larger back panel and attach them. Align the front with the lower end of the sides before you fasten it down.

Then Drill or cut the hole in the front panel according to the size preferred by the species you want to attract. House wrens, nuthatches, titmice and downy woodpeckers like small holes of about 1¼ in. diameter. Tree swallows, house finches, bluebirds, hairy woodpeckers and house sparrows prefer 1½ in. openings. Locate the hole 4–6 in. above the floor for most birds. With the panel resting on a block of scrap wood, drill the hole from the front to prevent splintering. For large houses with low entrances, drill 2 or 3 ventilation holes ¼ in. in diameter above the opening to let heat out.

Last For easy cleaning, hinge the roof to the back panel. Make sure the roof overhangs both sides and the front. Use a brass or galvanized steel hinge centered along the top. Fasten the hinge so that the roof fits as tightly as possible over the sides and front. Secure the roof with a brass latch to prevent the wind from lifting it. If you want to paint or stain the house, use natural colors such as light brown, green or gray. Avoid dark colors; they absorb heat.

Growing a Birdhouse

Amazing Gourds

Birds take advantage of all sorts of housing opportunities, including wooden boxes, moss baskets and even pipes and gutters. One alternative you can offer is a birdhouse made from a gourd grown in your vegetable garden. Children especially enjoy growing this gourd and turning it into a unique nesting site.

Gourds are fruits with hard, sometimes bumpy shells and interesting amber patterns or bright green and yellow stripes. Planted in the spring, the birdhouse gourd matures in early fall. Left to dry over several months in a warm, protected spot it will become hollow.

This annual vine is very easy to grow from seed. Plant seeds in early spring after the danger of frost has passed. Set the seeds one inch deep in hills six feet apart. Give the plants room to spread and climb. Birdhouse gourds grow in average garden soil and require sun and moderate amounts of water. Watch as the white five-petaled flowers fade and the bright green pear-shaped gourds form and enlarge. The vine itself is pretty, with multiple stems covered in velvety green leaves that reach ten inches across.

The plant will send out several twining stems that attach to anything, even adjoining plants. Use a trellis, arbor or fence to keep the vine in bounds. Support is important for the vine, because the gourds become quite heavy (up to ten pounds each). On a vigorous plant you can expect ten gourds or more.

This birdhouse gourd is a vigorous summer vine that spreads and climbs over several feet. Tie long stems to trellises or fences.

From Gourd to Birdhouse

First Harvest the gourd before the first frost when it has turned from green to tan. Leave several inches of stem to later hang it by. Lay the gourd on a screen or wooden flat to dry, and store it in a warm, dry, airy place. It may take several months to completely dry and become hollow. When dry the seeds will rattle inside. Wash the gourd with soapy water and dry it thoroughly.

Third To attract wrens, which like hanging houses, make a 1½ in. entrance hole 4–6 in. from the bottom of the gourd. Use a utility knife to cut the circular opening. Make several small angular cuts with the knife tip, then flip out the cut circle. Insert a wooden spoon handle to break up the fibers and seeds inside, then shake them free.

Then Coat the entire gourd with shellac, wax or paint. Let it dry overnight, then apply a second coat. This preserves the tough skin, waterproofs the gourd and keeps it from rotting. Birds prefer natural colors such as green, brown, gray or tan.

Last Attach wire securely to the stem and hang the gourd in a tree where cats and other predators cannot reach it. Wrens prefer houses 6–10 ft. above the ground. Face the gourd slightly downward to keep out rain.

FEEDING BIRDS

SEEDS & OTHER FOODS

Supplementing the birds' natural diet with seeds, fruit and suet or other fats can help them survive when other foods are scarce, particularly in late fall and winter when snow covers the ground.

Set up feeders in the fall in areas protected from cats or other predators. Check supplies regularly. A popular feeder may need refilling once or twice a day. It's important to be consistent because the birds will come to depend on the food you offer. When spring returns and natural food supplies are again available, discontinue regular feeding. This way birds teach their young to find natural food sources.

What to stock depends on which birds you're feeding. Most likely you'll have seed eaters—finches, sparrows, nuthatches, grosbeaks, titmice, towhees, cardinals, jays and others—that will come to wooden or plastic feeders with seed hoppers or trays. Commercial seed mixes are convenient, or you can prepare your own mix using sunflower seeds, thistle, cracked corn or peanut hearts. Where possible, clean up seed spillage, which may attract squirrels and other rodents and may contain weed seeds.

Fruit will attract mockingbirds, orioles, finches, woodpeckers, robins, catbirds and others. Suet—beef or other animal fat—provides energy to keep birds warm during the winter months and is especially attractive to woodpeckers, finches, cardinals and other insect eaters. Special wire or mesh feeders hold hardened suet cakes. Nuts are also popular. Peanuts can be strung in their shells on wires, combined with other nuts in mesh bags or scattered on a bird table affixed to a wooden post.

Seed eaters such as sparrows and siskins are attracted to this hanging wooden bird feeder, which holds a generous supply of birdseed, and will also eat seed on the ground.

Bird Feeders

Plastic seed feeders are light, inexpensive and effective for attracting many birds. It's best to include two or more feeders in the yard with different seed mixes, such as wild birdseed and sunflower seed. Select feeders that will keep the seed dry because wet, moldy seed can harm birds. Mount feeders on level 5-ft. posts or poles or suspend them from tree limbs. Refill feeders as often as necessary, especially in fall and winter when other food is scarce.

Suet is an excellent food for quick energy and warmth in cold months. Just about all garden birds, particularly insect eaters, eat suet. Netted bags and simple wire or mesh holders are perfect for suet cakes or chunks, as long as the wire is sturdy and won't entangle the birds' feet. For an irresistible suet cake, melt the suet and add sunflower seeds, bread crumbs, cornmeal and sand for grit. Pour it into plastic containers or tins to harden, then hang the cakes in the garden.

Baskets filled with seed and placed on decks, patios, porches or balconies will attract ground feeders such as finches, mourning doves, jays and juncos. A ground feeding station can be as simple as a cleared spot of earth. Locate feeding stations in open areas away from cat hiding places. Clear away wet seed after rains and add sand for grit to help birds digest food.

Fruit is an especially welcome food source in winter when natural supplies have dwindled. Add raisins and small pieces of dried fruit to feeding trays. Special feeders hold apples, oranges or other fruits on wooden dowels or plastic holders covered with clear domes. Be sure the fruit doesn't become moldy, and thoroughly clean any feeders that have had mold before restocking them.

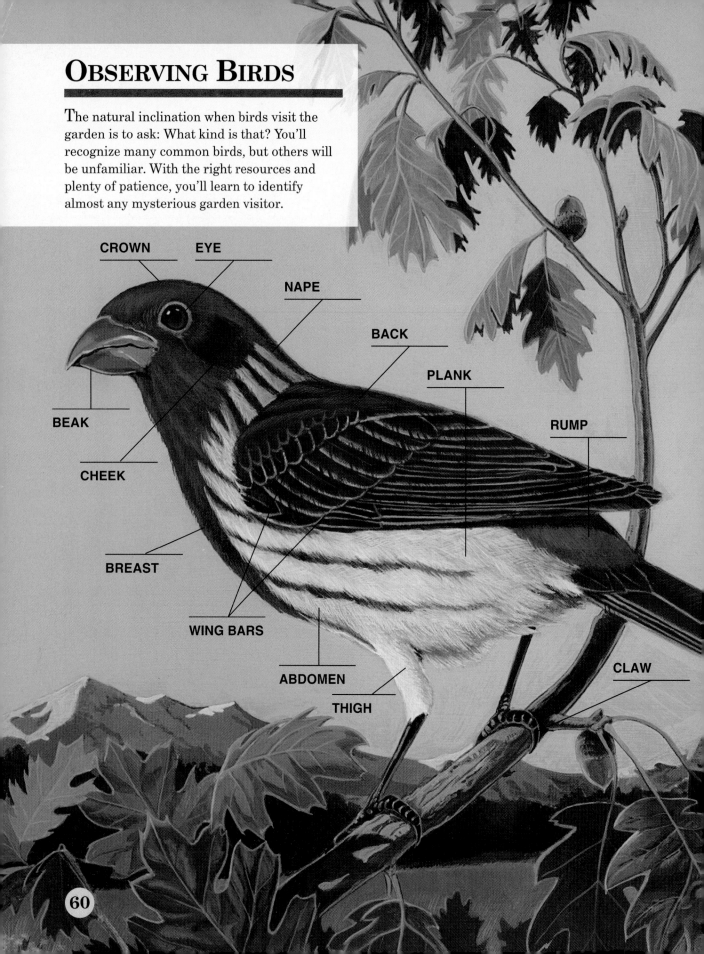

OBSERVING BIRDS

The natural inclination when birds visit the garden is to ask: What kind is that? You'll recognize many common birds, but others will be unfamiliar. With the right resources and plenty of patience, you'll learn to identify almost any mysterious garden visitor.

CROWN

EYE

NAPE

BACK

PLANK

BEAK

RUMP

CHEEK

BREAST

WING BARS

ABDOMEN

THIGH

CLAW

House Finch (*Carpodacus mexicanus*)

TAIL

IDENTIFYING BIRDS

The basic tools for bird identification are binoculars, a field guide and a notebook.

You don't need fancy or expensive binoculars for bird watching, although lightweight, compact models are easier to handle. Those with a magnification power of eight (listed as 8X) are popular. The second number in the specification (after the magnification) represents the size of the lens in millimeters. An 8X50 pair has 8X magnification and a 50-millimeter lens.

Field guides are usually organized according to bird family, although those organized by appearance, habitat or geographical area can be helpful to novices. Color photos or illustrations and information on each species should include size, field marks, similar species, voice, habitat, range, food and nest. To get started, study the layout of the field guide, noting the placement of bird families and groupings for quick reference later.

Keep a small notebook handy. Often birds will disappear so quickly you won't get to look them up in the field guide, so noting key features such as size, shape, head and bill will help you identify them later. Records can also help you notice seasonal trends, feeding schedules and nesting behavior.

To identify a bird, start by comparing its size and shape to birds you recognize. Then observe its face for distinctive patterns, and its beak. Determine whether the bill is thick for seed cracking or narrow to catch insects. Note its overall shape and color and any obvious markings on the tail, head, rump, wings or breast. Listen carefully for the song and watch how the bird moves—does it run, hop or scratch the ground? Note where you see it and what it eats. Use the information to narrow the choices to a few similar species, then try to pick out the individual you're observing. You may find bird identification is not as simple as it seems, but with practice you'll gradually improve your skill.

61

COMMON BIRDS

POTENTIAL GUESTS

The more diverse your backyard habitat, the greater the variety of birds you'll attract.

A backyard with a variety of deciduous and evergreen trees will attract species that prefer a forest habitat, such as nuthatches, siskins and some woodpeckers. An open, sunny area will attract open-country birds, such as mockingbirds and goldfinches. The edge between these two types of areas will attract both types of birds.

If you've planted seed-bearing plants and stocked bird feeders with seeds in the cold months, you'll probably have doves, sparrows, finches, juncos, grosbeaks, towhees and, if you live in the eastern half of the country, cardinals. Seed eaters are identified mostly by the shape of their beaks. They have large conical bills adapted to seed cracking. These birds often feed on the ground, hopping in and out of shrubbery or foraging under bird feeders. Some, like the small American goldfinch, even land on flower stalks or hang from young tree limbs while extracting seeds. Feeding stations, bird tables and hanging feeders will attract many of these birds.

Insect eaters are likely to be well represented in the garden. Swallows, flycatchers, thrushes (including robins), warblers, wrens, titmice and chickadees are common insect eaters. It's a varied group, but most have slender, pointed beaks for extracting insects from holes and crevices. You may find this group flitting about trees and shrubs, gleaning insects from around flowers and foliage.

Fruit draws many species, including robins, cedar waxwings and mockingbirds. All are boldly colored, distinctive birds easy to identify and beautiful to watch. Nectar from flowers will bring orioles and hummingbirds.

Do You See These?

Robin The bright rusty breast and white eye ring give robins a distinctive appearance. They eat insects, worms and grubs and are attracted to the fruit of honeysuckle, pyracantha, cotoneaster, mulberry, dogwood, mountain ash and crabapple. Robins may breed in the garden, building mud-lined nests of grasses and twigs in tree crotches and on flat surfaces, including building ledges.

House Finch Males display bright red forehead, breast and rump with brown-streaked sides, females lack the red markings. Purple finches are similar in appearance. House finches and purple finches prefer seeds, fruits and berries but also take insects. They particularly like thistle and sunflower seeds. Attract them with thick shrubbery for nesting and with honeysuckle, elderberry, sycamore, willow, and marigold or nasturtium flowers.

Downy Woodpecker Small, not much larger than a sparrow, this woodpecker looks very much like the shyer hairy woodpecker, which is larger and has a noticeably longer beak. Downies primarily eat insects, but also take suet, seeds and nut meats at feeders. They also eat some berries. Attract them with Virginia creeper, mulberry, sumac, dogwood, willow, birch and oak.

Cardinal From Texas eastward you can attract the crested, bright red, black-masked cardinal. The male cardinal combines his showy plumage with a vigorous whistled song. Females and immatures have brownish pink bodies, pink bills and reddish tails and wings. Cardinals prefer ground feeding and visit bird feeders, berry bushes, grapes, honeysuckle, roses and viburnums. Primarily seed eaters, cardinals love sunflowers. They feed insects to their young.

American Goldfinch Bright yellow feathers accented with black markings characterize this little bird. During breeding season, males have brilliant plumage; females and youngsters are olive-colored. Often these birds travel in flocks, finding seeds (sunflower and thistle) and, during nesting, insects. Attract these birds with cosmos, zinnia, coreopsis, bachelor's button, sunflowers, various wildflowers and weeds.

Northern Mockingbird Few birds can match the spectacular song of the northern mockingbird. This flashy black, white and gray bird lives year-round in California, most southern states and as far north as Connecticut. You may see a mockingbird hunting insects in the lawn by rapidly raising its wings and flashing brilliant white patches or by fanning its tail. To attract mockingbirds, provide thick shrubbery for nesting and blackberries, rose, pyracantha, dogwood, manzanita or grapes for food.

ATTRACTING HUMMINGBIRDS

Possessing iridescent plumage, energetic behavior and a willingness to let humans get close, hummingbirds make engaging garden guests. That they happen to like nectar from a wide range of beautiful flowers simply makes the task of attracting these little jewels to the garden a pleasure.

FOOD & SHELTER

Hummingbirds are specialized creatures adapted to drinking nectar from tubular blossoms, which they help pollinate. For protein, they feed on insects. They need trees, shrubs and vines for shelter, shade and nesting.

Planting a variety of flowering trees, shrubs, annuals and perennials with successive bloom times will attract hummers over many months. Flowers are especially important in fall and, if you live in a warm climate, in winter. Bright red, pink and orange flowers are most attractive to hummingbirds.

Fuchsias are top-rated flowers for attracting hummingbirds. In many areas of the country, they are planted in hanging baskets. Sometimes grown as annuals in colder regions, these shrubs produce many elegant, multicolored flowers from spring through fall.

Other desirable plants include lantana, bottle brush, grevillea species and butterfly bush. Impatiens, lupine, scarlet sage and petunia are favored annuals; coral bells, columbine, red-hot poker, bee balm and beard tongue are the preferred perennials.

Eucalyptus trees provide both nectar and nesting sites, as do honeysuckle and trumpet creeper vines. Lichen, moss and other plants with down fibers offer nesting materials.

To feed hummingbirds provide a sugar-water solution in a one to four ratio; discontinue feeding in the fall if their migratory instincts take over. Do not use honey as a sweetener; it can be a medium for a fungus harmful to hummingbirds. Place feeders in shade, no more than 15 feet from cover and away from cat hiding places. Bee guards at the end of the feeder tube discourage these insects, while salad oil on wires suspending the feeder deters ants.

Keep the sugar solution fresh, not cloudy, and the feeder clean by cleaning it once a week at least. Thoroughly remove all mold, which can breed bacteria and present health risks to the birds.

Hummingbirds are delightful garden visitors, darting from flower to flower—here a columbine, *Aquilegia* species—in search of nectar.

IDENTIFYING BUTTERFLIES

COMPOUND EYE

SPIRACLE

OBSERVING BUTTERFLIES

Identifying butterflies can be challenging, especially for species that have many similar relatives. Skill in butterfly identification starts with a field guide that has color photos or drawings and descriptions of the butterfly, similar species, life cycle, range and habitat. Field guides are arranged differently, so look over several to see which kind best suits your style. A notebook is important for listing key features of the butterflies you see, the plants they visit and information like flight patterns and the date and time of the observation.

Search in sunny, open locations where flowers grow—gardens, meadows, weedy patches, parks—on days when the temperature is at least 60 °F. You may also find butterflies in shady areas where there are damp patches of earth. Most butterflies are easily approachable, especially if you move slowly and quietly.

Knowing what to look for helps greatly. First determine the size and shape of the butterfly. Note how the wings are set, shaped and divided. Look at the base color, and accent or outline colors, which are typically contrasting. Identify prominent markings—stripes, dots, zigzag lines, eye spots; count marks or patterns and note colors. Finally, use the plants the butterflies visit as clues. Cross-check your information with the field guide photos and text to narrow choices and finally identify individuals.

You may find moths in the garden. They are distinguishable from butterflies by their more feathery antennae, somewhat broader body, habit of resting with wings spread and, for many, nighttime flights.

The regal monarch butterfly is a favorite backyard visitor that migrates southward—sometimes as far as Mexico—in winter. Its larvae feed exclusively on milkweed.

ANTENNAE

LEGS

THORAX

FOREWING

HIND WING

ABDOMEN

67

COMMON BUTTERFLIES

BUTTERFLY FAMILIES

A good way to begin identification is to learn about butterfly families—groupings of species with similar characteristics. Skippers, though not true butterflies, make up a large category or superfamily. These little butterflies are easily identified by their thick bodies, small triangular wings and quick, darting flight.

Many common visitors are in the brush-footed group, which includes colorful fritillaries—reddish to copper butterflies with distinctive black or white dots, lines or zigzags. Checkerspots, patches and crescents are similar family members with brightly colored, boldly patterned wings. Also look for anglewings or tortoiseshells with orange-and-black patterns on distinctly divided wings with scalloped edges.

The swallowtail family are mostly large, brightly colored butterflies with narrow, pointed tips on the hind wings and bold patterns in yellow and black. Whites and sulphurs, another butterfly family, typically range from white to yellow and orange and include orange tip and marble butterflies. The gossamer-winged family includes the small hairstreaks, which like woodland areas, the bright coppers in reddish to purplish colors and the various blues (females are brownish) in gray to silvery hues. Metalmarks, satyrs, wood nymphs and monarchs are other commonly seen butterflies.

There are differences between males and females and within species in different regions. In general, females tend to be duller and more muted in color than males or may be a different color altogether. Field guides point out regional color or pattern variations.

Western Tiger Swallowtail Distinguished by bright black bands on a pale yellow background, this butterfly, along with its close relatives the tiger swallowtail and two-tailed tiger swallowtail, visits many habitats, including backyards and wooded areas. Host plants for caterpillars include willows, poplars, birches and other deciduous trees. Good nectar sources include verbena (shown here), thistle, butterfly bush, and honeysuckle.

Red Admiral One of the most widespread, striking and admired of all common backyard butterflies is the red admiral. The red admiral with distinctive black wings frequents open areas and woodland edges, drinking nectar from flowers including dianthus (shown here). Caterpillars eat nettles. White admirals are similar but without much red and live on deciduous trees in the Northeast.

West Coast Lady It's sometimes difficult to spot the differences between the west coast lady and the similar painted lady and American painted lady. All three have dusky bodies with orange-and-black wings and blue spots on the hind wings. These butterflies inhabit many areas, including gardens, fields and parks. Host plants include thistles, wildflowers, mallows and hollyhocks. Nectar sources include the butterfly bush, zinnias and other garden flowers.

Fiery Skipper Named for their energetic skipping flight, these butterflies are common in backyards, parks, open fields, wooded areas, roadsides, marshes, forests and weedy, grassy places. Checkered skippers have bluish centers and spotted brown, white and gray wings. Caterpillars feed on plants in the grass family. Good nectar plants for attracting skippers are lantana, zinnia, aster, statice, marigold and evening primrose (shown here).

Cabbage White This European native has colonized all of North America. It is similar to other whites, including the common or checkered white. You'll find the cabbage white and its relatives in gardens, open areas, parks and woodlands. Considered by some to be a pest, the cabbage white (and other whites) uses cabbage, cresses, mustard, nasturtium and similar plants for larval food and for nectar.

Mourning Cloak With a spread of its wings, this master of camouflage can instantly change from bark-like brownish gray to a shimmering black with bands of blue and yellow. Common throughout the United States, it inhabits open areas, woodlands, forest borders, gardens and parks. Mourning cloaks prefer willow, aspen, ash and other deciduous trees as host plants and take nectar from butterfly bush, milkweed, other garden flowers and rotting fruit.

RAISING BUTTERFLIES

One of the best ways to observe and understand butterflies is to raise them at home in simple cages you can build. Collect caterpillars in the garden or send for larvae by mail. Provide them with the proper host food, and watch as they turn into perhaps the most wonderful of all garden guests.

This pipevine swallowtail butterfly, shown in a home-made cage, has given us an intimate look at the miracle transformation from cater-pillar to beautiful adult.

Creating a Home for Caterpillars

First A wooden box with somewhat rough surfaces, similar to those used to package wine, produce or other goods, makes a perfect cage for raising butterflies. Remove the lid and replace it with a snug-fitting sheet of glass or plastic. Drill 1-in. air holes in the sides and cover them with fine mesh or screen. Insert a raised wooden floor panel with a circular hole large enough to accommodate a small jar or potted plant. The jar, which will hold larval plant cuttings, should just reach the hole.

Then Collect caterpillars in the backyard or in nearby areas after checking local regulations. If you're lucky, you may spot a female laying eggs on a tree leaf. If so, put the leaf in water in the cage and wait for the eggs to hatch. Check them daily to see if the tiny caterpillars poke their black heads out. In spring or summer the caterpillars may emerge within a week. When they do, carefully place the larval food inside the cage.

Third Monitor the progress and appetite of the hungry caterpillars daily. You may need to add larval food frequently. Do this with great care, making sure to remove any caterpillars from the chewed stems you discard. If you have the larval food in a jar, place cotton around the opening to prevent the caterpillars from falling into the water. Change the water regularly. If the larval plant is growing in a pot, watch to see that its leaves aren't stripped and keep a second plant available as a replacement.

Last Soon the caterpillars are ready to spin a silken pad or band that holds the chrysalis in a nearly immobile state as metamorphosis begins. When the transformation is complete, the skin of the chrysalis will split open and the new butterfly, with frail wings and a shriveled body, will crawl out. It will pump fluid to the wings, which gradually spread and stiffen to their maximum size. This is its adult stage.

GOING BEYOND
THE GARDEN

LEARNING MORE

Once you create a garden that attracts birds and butterflies, you may want to know more about these entertaining garden guests. One excellent way to learn about wildlife is to visit public gardens, nature centers and museums.

Start by investigating what facilities are available in your area. Telephone directories often list public gardens, parks and museums in the "Places to Go" section. Sometimes local universities or big city parks have arboretums or botanical gardens with well-informed caretakers or volunteers. Occasionally, private businesses have outstanding gardens on their grounds and allow visitors.

Museums and nature centers sometimes have local species of birds or butterflies mounted on display or depicted in drawings or posters, which may help you identify individuals that visit your garden. Local experts are a wonderful source. Check with your local chapter of the National Audubon Society or bird club to find out about meetings, field trips and lectures.

Three outstanding butterfly gardens are located in the United States. Butterfly World in Coconut Creek, Florida, has native and exotic species in two screened aviaries. Butterfly World at Marine World Africa USA in Vallejo, California, has a glass rain forest-type of greenhouse with imported and unusual species. Day Butterfly Center at Calloway Gardens in Pine Mountain, Georgia, is the largest glass-enclosed butterfly conservatory in North America, and it is coupled with an outdoor garden designed to attract native species.

Public gardens, like this one at the Coyote Point Museum for Environmental Education, just south of San Francisco, California, are wonderful sources of information on local species and the plants that attract them.

PLANT REFERENCE CHART

COMMON NAME	BOTANICAL NAME	USED BY			USED FOR					
		Birds	Butterflies	Hummingbirds	Berries	Nectar	Fruit	Seeds	Shelter	Flowers
TREES										
Alder	Alnus glutinosa	•						•	•	
Almond	Prunus dulcis	•	•				•		•	•
American beech	Fagus grandifolia	•	•	•			•		•	
American mountain ash	Sorbus americana	•	•		•		•		•	•
American sweet gum	Liquidambar styraciflua	•						•	•	
Birch	Betula species	•	•	•				•	•	
Common hackberry	Celtis occidentalis	•	•		•		•		•	
Crabapple	Malus species	•				•	•		•	•
Elm	Ulmus species	•	•		•		•		•	
Fir	Abies species	•	•	•				•	•	
Flowering dogwood	Cornus florida	•			•		•		•	•
Maple	Acer species	•		•				•	•	
Oak	Quercus species	•	•					•	•	
Pine	Pinus species	•	•					•	•	
Red horse chestnut	Aesculus carnea			•		•			•	•
Southern magnolia	Magnolia grandiflora	•	•				•		•	•
Spruce	Picea species	•	•	•				•	•	
Tulip tree	Liriodendron tulipifera	•		•		•		•		•
Washington thorn	Crataegus phaenopyrum	•	•	•			•		•	•
Weeping willow	Salix babylonica	•	•	•					•	
SHRUBS										
Cinquefoil	Potentilla fruticosa		•			•				•
Common butterfly bush	Buddleia davidii	•	•	•		•				•
Cotoneaster	Cotoneaster species	•	•	•	•	•				•
English holly	Ilex aquifolium	•			•				•	
Firethorn	Pyracantha species	•			•				•	•
Flowering quince	Chaenomeles species			•		•				•
Fountain butterfly bush	Buddleia alternifolia	•	•	•		•				•
Fuchsia	Fuchsia hybrida			•		•				
Japanese barberry	Berberis thunbergii	•			•				•	
Juniper	Juniperus species	•		•			•	•	•	
Lantana	Lantana species	•	•	•	•	•				•
Lilac	Syringa species	•	•	•		•				•
Manzanita	Arctostaphylos species	•					•	•	•	•
Rose	Rosa species	•		•			•		•	•
Spiraea	Spiraea x bumalda	•	•			•			•	•
Sweet mock orange	Philadelphus coronarius	•	•			•			•	•

	PLANT HEIGHT						LIGHT			SOIL					FOOD SOURCE				USES						
	Under 3 ft.	3–6 ft.	6–12 ft.	12–20 ft.	20–30 ft.	Over 30 ft.	Sun	Partial Sun	Shade	Sandy Soil	Clay Soil	Dry Soil	Moist Soil	Well-drained Soil	Spring	Summer	Fall	Winter	Accent	Color	Border	Screen	Background	In Groupings	Containers
					•	•	•			•			•	•				•					•		•
				•			•			•		•		•	•		•							•
					•	•			•			•	•			•						•		•
				•		•	•		•											•				•
					•	•				•		•	•	•		•		•	•			•		•
					•	•			•	•		•	•	•		•	•							•
					•	•			•	•	•	•	•			•	•					•		•
		•	•	•		•				•		•	•	•		•	•		•					•
					•	•			•			•	•	•	•	•	•							•
					•	•			•			•	•			•						•	•	•
				•		•	•		•			•	•			•		•	•				•	•
			•	•	•	•	•		•	•		•	•	•	•	•		•	•			•	•	•
					•	•			•	•	•	•	•	•	•	•		•	•			•	•	•
		•	•	•	•	•			•			•	•	•	•		•	•	•			•	•	•
					•	•			•	•		•	•	•		•		•	•			•		
					•	•				•		•	•	•	•	•						•		
					•	•			•	•		•	•			•						•	•	•
					•	•				•		•	•	•		•		•	•			•		
				•		•			•	•	•	•	•	•	•	•	•	•	•			•	•	
					•	•			•	•		•					•				•	•	•	
•	•					•			•		•		•	•						•			•	
	•	•				•	•		•	•		•	•		•	•		•	•				•	•
•	•	•	•			•			•	•		•	•	•	•		•	•	•		•	•	•	•
			•	•	•		•	•	•			•				•	•		•			•	•	
		•	•			•				•	•	•			•	•			•			•	•	
	•	•				•			•	•		•	•	•		•		•	•			•		
	•	•				•	•		•	•		•	•			•			•				•	
•	•						•	•	•			•		•		•			•				•	•
	•					•	•		•	•		•	•			•			•			•	•	
•	•	•	•	•	•	•			•	•		•	•			•					•	•	•	•
•	•					•			•	•	•	•	•	•	•	•		•	•	•	•		•	
		•	•			•			•	•		•	•	•				•	•			•	•	•
•	•	•	•	•		•			•	•		•	•			•	•	•	•				•	
•	•	•				•			•	•		•	•			•	•	•	•	•	•		•	•
	•					•	•			•		•	•		•	•				•		•		•
		•				•	•			•		•	•	•				•	•			•		

PLANT REFERENCE CHART
(continued)

COMMON NAME	BOTANICAL NAME	USED BY			USED FOR					
		Birds	Butterflies	Hummingbirds	Berries	Nectar	Fruit	Seeds	Shelter	Flowers
SHRUBS *(continued)*										
Viburnum	Viburnum species	•			•	•		•		•
Weigela	Weigela species			•		•			•	•
Western serviceberry	Amelanchier alnifolia	•				•	•			•
Wild lilac	Ceanothus species	•	•	•		•			•	•
ANNUALS & PERENNIALS										
Ageratum	Ageratum houstonianum	•	•			•		•		•
Alyssum, sweet	Lobularia maritima		•			•				•
Bachelor's button	Centaurea cyanus	•	•			•		•		•
Bee balm	Monarda didyma		•	•		•				•
Butterfly weed	Aesclepias tuberosa		•			•				•
Columbine	Aquilegia species			•		•				•
Coralbells	Heuchera sanguinea			•		•				•
Coreopsis	Coreopsis species	•	•			•		•		•
Cosmos	Cosmos bipinnatus	•	•			•		•		•
Delphinium	Delphinium species		•	•		•				•
Dianthus	Dianthus species		•			•				•
Goldenrod	Solidago species	•				•		•		•
Hollyhock	Alcea rosea		•			•				•
Marigold	Tagetes species	•	•			•		•		•
Nasturtium	Tropaeolum majus		•			•				•
Nicotiana	Nicotiana species		•	•		•				•
Penstemon	Penstemon species		•	•		•				•
Purple coneflower	Echinacea purpurea		•			•		•		•
Sunflower	Helianthus annuus	•						•		•
Wallflower	Erysimum linifolium		•			•				•
VINES & GROUND COVERS										
Bearberry and manzanita	Arctostaphylos species	•		•		•	•			•
Cape honeysuckle	Tecomaria capensis			•		•				•
Cardinal climber	Ipomoea x multifida			•		•				•
Grape	Vitis species	•					•			•
Honeysuckle	Lonicera species	•	•	•	•	•			•	•
Ivy	Hedera species	•					•		•	
Raspberry and loganberry	Rubus species	•					•		•	
Strawberry	Fragaria chiloensis	•				•				•
Trumpet creeper	Campsis species			•		•			•	•
Virginia creeper	Parthenocissus quinquefolia	•				•			•	

	PLANT HEIGHT						LIGHT			SOIL					FOOD SOURCE				USES						
	Under 3 ft.	3–6 ft.	6–12 ft.	12–20 ft.	20–30 ft.	Over 30 ft.	Sun	Partial Sun	Shade	Sandy Soil	Clay Soil	Dry Soil	Moist Soil	Well-drained Soil	Spring	Summer	Fall	Winter	Accent	Color	Border	Screen	Background	In Grouping	Containers
		•	•				•	•		•	•		•	•	•		•	•	•	•	•	•	•	•	•
		•	•				•	•			•		•	•	•	•				•	•	•	•		
			•	•			•	•		•	•	•	•	•	•	•						•	•	•	
		•	•	•	•		•			•	•	•		•	•	•		•		•		•	•	•	
	•						•	•		•			•	•	•	•	•			•	•			•	•
	•						•	•		•	•	•	•	•	•	•	•	•		•	•			•	•
	•						•	•		•			•	•		•				•	•			•	•
	•						•	•		•			•	•		•				•	•			•	
	•						•			•	•	•		•		•				•	•			•	
	•						•	•		•	•		•	•	•	•				•	•			•	
	•						•	•		•	•		•	•	•	•				•	•			•	•
	•						•			•	•	•	•	•	•	•	•			•	•			•	•
	•	•					•			•	•		•	•		•	•			•	•			•	
	•	•					•	•		•			•	•		•			•	•	•			•	
	•						•			•			•	•	•	•				•	•				•
	•						•			•	•		•	•	•	•	•			•	•			•	
	•	•					•			•	•		•	•	•	•	•		•	•	•			•	
	•						•			•	•		•	•		•	•			•	•			•	•
	•						•	•		•	•		•	•	•	•	•			•	•				•
	•						•	•		•	•	•	•	•	•	•			•	•	•			•	
	•						•			•	•		•	•	•	•				•	•			•	
	•						•			•	•		•	•	•	•	•			•	•			•	
	•						•			•	•		•	•		•				•	•			•	
		•	•				•				•		•	•		•	•		•	•		•			
	•						•	•		•			•	•	•	•				•	•				•
	•						•			•		•	•	•	•		•	•						•	•
				•			•			•			•	•	•	•	•	•		•		•			
				•			•			•		•		•						•					
				•			•				•					•	•					•			
				•			•	•			•		•	•	•	•	•			•		•			
					•		•	•	•	•	•		•	•	•		•	•		•					
		•					•			•				•		•				•	•		•		
	•						•			•					•	•								•	
				•			•	•	•		•		•	•		•	•					•		•	
					•		•	•	•		•		•	•			•	•		•	•		•		

INDEX

A

Aalcea species, 35
ageratum (*Ageratum houstonianum*), 28
American goldfinch, 63
annuals
    for birds, 18-19
    installing, 42-43
    nectar-rich, 28-29
annual vines, 17
Aquilegia species, 19
Arctostaphylos species, 21
Armeria species, 29
Asclepias tuberosa, 29

B

bachelor's button (*Centaurea cyanus*), 18
backyard ponds, 52-53
base garden plan, 36
beauty bush (*kolkwitzia amabilis*), 31
bee balm (*Monarda didyma*), 19
beneficial insects, 48
berries, 20-21
binoculars, 61
birdbaths, 51
birdhouse gourd, 56-57
birdhouses
    building, 54-55
    growing a, 56-57
bird nesting, 22-23
birds
    attracting, 10
    attracting hummingbirds, 64-65
    benefits of, 7
    berries for, 20-21
    common, 62-63
    feeding, 58-59
    flowers for, 18-19
    grasses for, 16-17
    insect control by, 48
    observing, 60-61
    shrubs for, 14-15
    trees for, 12-13
    vines for, 16-17

water for, 50-51
birdwatching, 60-61
Briza media, 33
broadleaf evergreen trees, 13
bubble diagrams, 37
Buddleia alternifolia, 30
Buddleia davidii, 30
bumalda spiraea shrub (*Spiraea* x *bumalda*), 31
butterflies
    attracting, 24-25
    benefits of, 6
    common families of, 68-69
    identifying, 66-67
    life cycle of, 26-27
    raising, 70
    shrubs for, 30-31
    trees and grasses for, 32-33
    water for, 50-51
    See also caterpillars
butterfly weed (*Asclepias tuberosa*), 29
Butterfly World garden (Coconut Creek), 73
Butterfly World garden (Marine World Africa USA), 73

C

cabbage white butterfly, 69
Campsis radicans, 17
candytuft (*Iberis sempervirens*), 29
cane berries, 20
cardinal, 63
cardinal climber (*Ipomoea quamoclit*), 17
caterpillars
    creating home for, 71
    feeding, 34-35
    life cycle of, 27
    trees for, 32-33
    See also butterflies
Centaurea cyanus, 18
Chinese elm (*Ulmus parvifolia*), 33
chrysalises, 27

Chrysanthemum x *superbum,* 29
cinquefoils (*Potentilla* species), 35
columbine (*Aquilegia* species), 19
common butterfly bush (*Buddleia davidii*), 30
compost, 40-41
conifers, 13
coral bells (*Heuchera sanguinea*), 19
coreopsis (*Coreopsis verticillata*), 19
Cornus florida, 33
cosmos (*Cosmos bipinnatus/Cosmos sulphureus*), 18
cotoneaster (*Cotoneaster* species), 20
Crataegus species, 34
Crataegus phaenopyrum, 21

D

Day Butterfly Center (Calloway Gardens), 73
deciduous shrubs, 15
deciduous trees, 13
delphiniums (*Delphinium elatum*), 19
dianthus (*Dianthus chinensis*), 28
disease, 49
downy woodpecker, 63

E

Echinacea purpurea, 29
Erysimum linifolium, 29
evergreen ground covers, 17
evergreen shrubs, 15
evergreen vines, 17

F

fall garden maintenance, 46
fertilizing, 45
fescues (*Festuca* species), 17, 35
fiery skipper butterfly, 69

flowering dogwood (*Cornus florida*), 33
flowering shrubs, 15
flowering tobacco (*Nicotiana* species), 29
flowering trees, 13
flowering viburnums shrub (*Virburnum tinus*), 31
flowers
    for birds, 18-19
    nectar-rich, 28-29
Forsythia x *interrnedia,* 15
fountain butterfly bush (*Buddleia alternifolia*), 30
fountains, 51
Fragaria chiloensis, 17
fruiting shrubs, 15
fruit trees, 12
fuchsias, 65

G

garden design, 8, 36-37
gardens
    attracting butterflies to, 24-25
    benefits of ecological, 6-7
    creating bird and butterfly, 8-9
    installing plants in, 42-43
    installing water, 53
    natural evolvement of, 9
    public, 73
    routine maintenance of, 9, 44-45
    sample, 38-39
    seasonal care for, 46-47
    shelter requirements for, 11
    water as essential element in, 50-51
golden bells (*Forsythia* x *interrnedia*), 15
goldenrod (*Solidago hybrids*), 19
grasses
    for butterflies, 32-33
    as caterpillar host plants, 35

grooming gardens, 45
ground covers
  berry producing, 21
  for birds, 16-17

H

hardening seeds, 42
hawthorne (*Crataegus* species), 34
hedges, 11
Helianthus annuus, 19
Heuchera sanguinea, 19
hollyhock (*Alcea* species), 35
honeysuckle vines (*Lonicera* species), 16
house finch, 62
hummingbirds
  attracting, 64
  food and shelter for, 65
  See also birds

I

Iberis sempervirens, 29
Indian grass (*Molinia caerulea*), 33
insect control, 48
Ipomoea multifida, 17

J

Jasminum officinale, 17
Juniperus chinensis
  `Pfilzerana' species, 15

K

kolkwitzia amabilis, 31

L

lantana shrub (*Lantana montevidensis*), 31
lilac (*Syringa vulgaris*), 31
lobelia (*Lobelia erinus*), 28
Lobularia maritima, 29
loganberry (*Rubus ursinus*), 20
Lonicera species, 16

M

maintenance
  seasonal garden, 46-47
  types of routine, 9, 44-45
marigolds, 18
Mexican feathergrass, 32

Molinia caerulea, 33
monarch butterfly, 66-67
Monarda didyma, 19
moor grass (*Molinia caerulea* grass), 35
mourning cloak butterfly, 69
mulching, 44

N

nasturtiums (*Tropaeolum majus*), 19
nectar-rich flowers, 28-29
needled evergreen trees, 13
nesting (bird), 22-23
Nicotiana species, 29
northern mockingbird, 63
nut trees, 12

O

ornamental strawberry (*Fragaria chiloensis*), 17

P

perennials
  for birds, 19
  installing, 42-43
  nectar-rich, 29
perennial vines, 17
pesticides, 48
Pfilzer juniper (*Juniperus chinensis* `Pfilzerana'), 15
pipevine swallowtail butterfly, 70
ponds, 52-53
Populus species, 35
Potentilla species, 35
pruning, 45
public gardens, 73
purple coneflower (*Echinacea purpurea*), 29
purple moor grass (*Molinia caerulea*), 33
pyracantha (*Pyracantha angustifolia*), 15

Q

quaking grass (*Briza media*), 33

R

red admiral butterfly, 68

robin, 62

S

St. Augustine grass (*Stenotaphrum secundatum*), 35
Salix babylonica, 32
sea pink (*Armeria* species), 29
seasonal maintenance, 46-47
seeds
  growing plants from, 42-43
  to supplement bird diet, 58-59
shasta daisy (*Chrysanthemum* x *superbum*), 29
sheep's fescue (*festuca ametina*), 17
shelter requirements, 11
shrubs
  benefits of, 11
  berry, 20
  for birds, 14-15
  for butterflies, 25, 30-31
  for hummingbirds, 65
site (garden), 8, 36
skipper butterfly, 69
soil
  improving the, 40-41
  preparation steps for, 9
Solidago hybrids, 19
special garden features, 9
Spiraea x *bumalda,* 31
spring garden maintenance, 46
Stenotaphrum secundatum, 35
stipa (*Stipa gigantea*), 32
summer garden maintenance, 46
sunflowers (*Helianthus annuus*), 19
swallowtail butterfly, 68
sweet alyssum (*Lobularia maritima*), 29
Syringa vulgaris, 31

T

trees
  benefits of, 11
  berry producing, 21

for birds, 12-13
  for butterflies, 25, 32-33
  for hummingbirds, 65
Tropaeolum majus, 19
trumpet vine (*Campsis radicans*), 17

U

Ulmus parvifolia, 33

V

verbena (*Verbena* x *hybrida*), 29
viburnum (*Viburnum* species), 20
vines
  benefits of, 11
  for birds, 16-17

W

wallflower (*Erysimum linifolium*), 29
Washington thorn tree (*Crataegus phaenopyrum*), 21
water
  creating backyard ponds, 52-53
  as essential garden element, 50-51
  to attract birds, 10
  to attract butterflies, 24
water garden, 53
watering, 44
weeding, 45
west coast lady butterfly, 69
western tiger swallowtail butterfly, 68
white jasmine (*Jasminum officinale*), 17
willows (*Salix babylonica*), 32
winter garden maintenance, 47

Z

zinnias (*Zinnia elegans*), 19

A NOTE FROM NK LAWN & GARDEN CO.

For more than 100 years, since its founding in Minneapolis, Minnesota, NK Lawn & Garden has provided gardeners with the finest quality seed and other garden products.

We doubt that our leaders, Jesse E. Northrup and Preston King, would recognize their seed company today, but gardeners everywhere in the United States still rely on NK Lawn & Garden's knowledge and experience at planting time.

We are pleased to be able to share this practical experience with you through this ongoing series of easy-to-use gardening books.

Here you'll find hundreds of years of gardening experience distilled into easy-to-understand text and step-by-step pictures. Every popular gardening subject is included.

As you use the information in these books, we hope you'll also try our lawn and garden products. They're available at your local garden retailer.

There's nothing [...]
successful, beautiful [...]
something special [...]
blooming flowers a [...]
grown garden vege[...]

We understand [...]
growing things—an[...]
feels the same way, [...]
a friend to gardene[...]